REPOSSIBLE BOX SET 2 (BOOKS 6-8)

DECIDE, MEDITATE, SPARK

BRADLEY CHARBONNEAU

CONTENTS

Introduction   ix

DECIDE

Preface   13
Prologue   15
Foreword   17

PART I
THINK

1. Introduction   23
2. Oops, that's one decision already   26
3. A smidgen of a glance at the seed of a thought   28
4. Not simple and not easy   30
5. What was that tingle in the hairs on the back of your neck?   33

PART II
DOUBT

6. Introduction   37
7. The school uniform and unleashing massive brain power   39
8. Let's decide this better together   42
9. The tiny little secret of the tipping point   44

PART III
DECIDE

10. Introduction   49
11. Decide and people will come   51
12. Simple but not easy   54
13. Relief   56

PART IV
FLOW

14. Introduction   61

15. Decisions beget decisions	62
16. The big decisions will help guide the smaller decisions	64
17. When you change your mind, you change your mind	68

PART V
PLAY

18. Introduction	73
19. Give a voice to your truth and a truth to your voice	74
20. Why don't they teach this in school? Or anywhere?	77
21. When are decisions triggered in the subconscious minds of children?	79
22. Simple and easy	81
23. Snowball	83

PART VI
POSTSCRIPT

24. Decide U.	87
25. Every Single Day	89
Did any part of this book help you in any way?	91
Relationship	93
About the Author	95
The End	97
Also by Bradley Charbonneau	99

MEDITATE

Introduction	115
Prologue	117
Preface	119

PART I
THIS WILL ONLY TAKE 17 MINUTES

1. Here's How to Meditate	123
2. Guided Meditation Audio: Clarity	125
3. It's OK to Have Fun Along the Way	126
4. Go it alone. Do it together.	129
5. Make Your Own News	131
6. Guided Meditation Audio: Creativity	134

PART II
WHY BOTHER?

7. The best time to plant a tree was 20 years ago	137
8. A Cascade Throughout the Day	140
9. Thank You, Thank You, Thank You	143
10. The Cult of You	145

PART III
IT'S NOT ME, IT'S YOU

11. YOU are the subject of this book, after all	153
12. Relax	155
13. "Between you and me, Bradley..."	158
14. From 1-Minute Meditations in the Bus to Solving World Problems	161
15. Talk to People Who Meditate	163

PART IV
EVERY SINGLE DAY

16. When 30 days is not quite enough	167
17. Food is a Factor	170
18. One Idea Per Day	172
19. Numbers, proof, and action	174
20. Candlelight Dinner on the Eiffel Tower	176
21. The Passion to _____ Has to be Greater than the Fear of _____	180
22. The Radio Signal is Always Transmitting	182

PART V
SO THIS HAPPENED

23. Out of the Spiritual Closet	187
24. Oh Deer	189
25. Rupert	193
26. I'm a Drug Dealer	195
27. Tiny Keys Lodged in His Back	203

PART VI
NOW WHAT?

28. It's Time to Make Time	209
Epilogue	211
Acknowledgments	215

Relationship	217
About the Author	219
Also by Bradley Charbonneau	223
The End	226

SPARK

Prologue	239
Foreword	241

PART I
WHY

1. Introduction: Embers	245
2. The quarter-inch drill bit, sparks, and expectations	247
3. Message in a Bottle	249
4. Let's create a family tradition	251
5. Rina	253

PART II
WHO

6. Introduction: Campers	257
7. The Widow and the Orphan	259
8. Gavin	262
9. LIFO: Last In, First Out	266
10. Maggie	268

PART III
WHAT

11. Introduction: Fire	275
12. It's an Experiment	278
13. The Great Unknown	280
14. Craig	282
15. Create more than you consume	285
16. Arlene	288

PART IV
WHEN

17. Introduction: Kindling	295
18. It's Now or Never	297
19. Rich	300

20. Lizz	302
21. Lorena	304

PART V
HOW

22. Introduction: Sparks	309
23. Replace Car Engine in Two Steps	311
24. Halfway will never finish	313
25. Create a Conflict	314
26. Meg	317
27. Want to truly learn something? Learn it through your kids.	319
28. How to make friends and influence...your kids	323
29. Brad	326
30. Don't talk about the project. Start the project.	328
31. Keep it legal, but keep it real	331
32. Linda	334

PART VI
CAMPFIRE STORIES

33. Introduction: Matches	339
34. How to instill creativity in your children in three not-so-easy steps.	342
35. Loss leaders, sales, flea markets and 12-year olds who want new shoes.	345
36. Make money, teach your kids math, and clean the house...at the same time.	350
37. How would your own kid sell his own book?	355

PART VII
GLOW

38. Spark Campfire	361
39. Questions for Parents	363
Afterword	365
Acknowledgments	367
Relationship	369
About the Author	371
Also by Bradley Charbonneau	373
The End	375

INTRODUCTION

Welcome to the second Repossible box set!

If you've arrived here new to the series, here is the entire lineup to give you an idea of the Repossible Roadmap:

1. Repossible
2. Every Single Day
3. Ask
4. Dare
5. Create
6. **Decide**
7. **Meditate**
8. **Spark**
9. Surrender
10. Play
11. Celebrate
12. Evaluate
13. Elevate

The first book, Repossible, is an introduction to the series and the rest of the books.

Every Single Day is both an introduction to the case study of the first Repossible experiment as well as something of an autobiography.

Now we're at Decide, Meditate, and Spark. Each one very different yet crucial in the process.

Enjoy.

Bradley Charbonneau

BRADLEY CHARBONNEAU

DECIDE

THERE'S USUALLY A CHOICE... IT'S USUALLY YOURS

THE REPOSSIBLE SERIES
Your *Playful* Guide to Who will You be Next?

PRAISE FOR EVERY SINGLE DAY

"Deliciousness to My Soul"

— P.C. via Amazon

"This book saved me!"

— Paige

"I was skeptical. I didn't think a book could help to motivate me. Heck, I had purchased a different book and did not even finish it even though it had been a good one. **But then there is ESD.** Oh my goodness. **This is exactly what I needed for my inspiration, motivation, and really living my life around my goals!** This book presents new ways to frame ideas and how to go about making & achieving goals, living the life you want and deserve, and forming habits in a non-scary way. I can't sign up for a 'new habit in 100 days,' but I can absolutely get behind the doing something each day method. **I couldn't put this down.** The language & material are great for one to kind of fly through as desired. I actually read through it once, then have gone back to specific sections for re-reading & review. I am keeping this on my night table for easy access and as a reminder for the tools I've learned and how to build upon them. So many things I have wanted to do in life and this books has made me feel they are all possible. Not just for 'I want to climb Mt Everest someday.' This is for your everyday. For You. For whatever the smallest or largest thing in your life is, I can't recommend this enough. **Don't think of it as a self-help book. Think of it as your right-hand tool as you go through the steps to accomplish any of your goals!** Happy Reading!"

— Julie Pedersen

"Somehow, I found myself devouring this today. It's rare that I allow myself this indulgence as the list of what I need to be doing in my head is endless.

Deliciousness to my soul, is the description that comes to mind as I reflect on my experience of consuming this book. I have no idea how to write a review and put into words **how deeply this resonated within me.**

There's a spark within me that has been relit. I know **ESD is the kindling I need to get the fire crackling and roaring** ... there are flames here that need to breathe and light the world.

Thank you Bradley Charbonneau for accepting the challenge of ESD, so that today, you could influence my ESD."

— 5 stars from P.C. via Amazon

"**Before reading this book I was ashamed of myself.**

For years I had called myself an artist but I knew the truth. I was only masquerading as one. ... But could I continue to call myself an artist when I stoped making artwork? The answers is no.

I am not entirely sure what happened to me from the time I was in college until now, eight years later. There was **a shift that took place** in my mind during that time.

I **developed a fear** of making artwork. I would always make excuses as to why I just couldn't create. I was too tired, the dog needed a bath, I needed to do dishes. What was the point of painting anyway **because no one would want to buy or look at my work** etc.

I have spent many years working dead end jobs just to pay bills. **I never even allowed myself a chance** at having a career because I would give up at the slightest failure or rejection.

The few times I did really try, I won awards at competitions.

I now have a two-year-old son. I have used him as an

excuse to not make art for the past two years. **I feel guilty** that I put so much blame on my son. Taking care of him was just a convenient excuse that is easily believed by most people.

After reading this book, there is no going back. I have no choice.

I make artwork everyday and I am happy. ... I know there is no going back.

I was miserable with guilt and now I am not.

I was afraid to create and now I happy to learn once more.

When I started to draw again I was really rusty but I got through it. **I find time** even though I take care of my son all day and I babysit my nephew for eight and a half hours a day.

I wrote this review in the hope that I could inspire someone else to change their life.

Take the Every Single Day challenge. Read this book it just might change your life."

— Paige

"The author shows us how to get past "**analysis paralysis**" to actually start projects and see them through until completion.

A theme of this book is to **dream about doing something until the dream itself is internalized along with the willingness to progress toward goal completion in iterative steps taken each day.** Readers will learn the importance of getting past inertia in order to begin complex tasks and progress toward a completion date with certainty.

Everyone who moves toward a meritorious goal must first start, stumble, reassess and move ahead with a refined approach toward reaching the goals set forth at the outset. **Very few, if any, tasks are completed with zero failure points or stumbles.** A strong point of the book is that the author sets up readers for roadblocks which must be overcome as part of the learning process. The book could be labelled alternatively as "what it takes to succeed"!"

— Dr. Joseph S. Maresca, Amazon "Hall of Fame" Reviewer

"Maybe you've let your dreams rust.

Author Bradley Charbonneau has published several children's books and travel books, but in this 'self-help' genre he **unveils his own secrets for making life meaningful and successful.**

... the author opens the gates to his pathway for fulfillment and success. **'I transformed myself when I made the decision to change my behavior.'** He places bold statements throughout to make sure he has our attention, phrases such as **'Dreaming the dream was a whole lot easier than living the dream.'**

This fine book encourages us to take a very deep breath, start afresh, and make or lives what they CAN be. A very fine book."

— GRADY HARP, AMAZON "HALL OF FAME" TOP 100 REVIEWER

"A life changer.

See, I don't joke when reviewing a book.

This is a kind of book which

Tells about a particular productivity model

Explains about the benefits of the point and

Makes THE ADAPTATION easy - in case one chooses to follow

The author makes sure that the style is **lucid and easy to move with.**

Language is comfortable and the whole book is in a consumable fashion.

I look forward to read more productivity focused books from this author."

— CANDOAR

"This author has provided an excellent "how to" book, to **move past procrastination**, and **getting past fear** - teaching the reader how things made habitual can result in transformational success. This book could be **a really important read for the new, young person looking to "start" his life journey**, or switch directions after a rocky start. His writing is humorous, friendly, and engaging. I have bought two copies - one for both of my adult children."

— Robert Enzenauer

"A Game Changer."

— Dr. Beth Brombosz

" ... for anyone with **dreams hidden in the attic, cellar or heart.**"

— Amazon Reviewer

"If you're ready to **live your dream** (as compared with simply dreaming your dream), this book will help you do it."

— Laurie King

"I love how you handle **deep subjects in such a light-hearted way.**"

— Kay Bolden

I work with people who cannot see past their current situation. Yet, they want to become more than who they are today. This book is **a tool I will use to help reach my clients.**

— Tracy Gannaway, Physical Therapist

It feels like a clue, a hint, a hunt, **a push to make a mental leap I have not yet made as a business owner.**

— Kristen Desmond, Founder and CEO of Flagstone Pantry

"He lights a path that you can choose to walk down."

— Ray Simon, accomplished speaker, and a no-longer-secret trumpet player

For my Mom

Because at some point early on in my childhood she instilled in me the idea that who I would become was a choice and that choice was up to me.

PREFACE

"I didn't have time to write a short letter, so I wrote a long one instead."

— MARK TWAIN

I read a really long book recently and there were 14 different topics.

I forgot what most of them were.

The few I did remember were less solid because they were bogged down by the others I forgot about.

I'm shooting for a single topic and we can cover it succinctly and quickly.

I think it can be done and I'm going to do it. My strategy is to create shorter books with, ideally, one topic per book.

That's my decision.

See?

I've already made one.

It's going to make writing—and reading—this book easier, more efficient, and more effective.

And we're only in the Preface.

PROLOGUE

"My drummer, bass player, and guitar player sing backgrounds. They play and sing. I can sing all the harmonies, but I can't do it alone."

— Aaron Neville

*I*f you're reading this, you've already made a decision. Several, actually.

1. To see the cover,
2. Think about your challenges,
3. Buy this book,
4. Open it up,
5. Read this page.

That's already 5 decisions. We're only in the Prologue.

There's another decision that might change this book, future books, and your perspective on the future.

That might seem like a lot, but I'm asking, yep, early on in this book, to think about questions you have as you read, feedback, improvements, and your own opinion.

I'm seeking your feedback, comments that are only yours, ideas that might be hiding under the surface, experiences unique to you, case studies—anything that will make the book better for future readers who could benefit from the goodness that you'll (hopefully!) find inside these pages.

The stories in this book are mostly mine. That's fine and all, but they will be better if this book becomes "ours" instead of just "mine" or seen from your perspective, "his."

In return, I'll share early editions of my upcoming books, provide you with free or discounted rates, and, on your deathbed, you'll receive total consciousness.

(OK, 2 out of 3 isn't bad, right?)

Up for it?

Check out the following URL for extras, video, audio, and whatever else you and we can dream up to add even more value to the power of *Decide*.

decide.repossible.com

Without you, it's just me. Without you I'm just I. But with you, we're we and not just from my perspective, but from yours as well. I invite you to make this "we" instead of "me."

FOREWORD

There are 71 questions in this book. Bradley Charbonneau asks a lot of questions.

Along the way he also asked me to write this foreword to his latest book, *Decide, There's Usually a Choice. It's Usually Yours.* So I guess that makes 72 questions.

The reward for asking a lot of questions is people often decide to say yes to something you want. I decided to say yes for a ton of reasons, mostly for the joy of helping Bradley and some for the fun of telling parts of his story that he doesn't. A little bit risky on his part, if you ask me! Like asking the friend you'd spent a weekend in Vegas with to give a toast at your wedding.

Bradley is by far the most curious person I've ever met and having a curious friend means every conversation is an adventure.

For this author, every adventure is also a potential topic for his Every Single Day (ESD) habit of writing, now at day #2,165. Which is close to six years!

I don't know about you, but there aren't very many things beyond basic hygiene and sustenance I've done every single day for six years!

I met Bradley on #910 ESD. Within a few hours of meeting him I bluntly stated, "You will get me to write." Only a little pressure on my brand new acquaintance!

Turns out encouraging people to develop a writing habit, write books with their kids, and all things around creating and marketing books, only adds fuel to Bradley's Eternal Flame Falls.

In between discovering Charlie Holiday's superpowers and chasing lost balls through castles and caverns, Bradley supports writers with podcasts, and courses such as *Audio for Authors* and *How to Publish Your First Book*.

Like the *Eternal Flame Falls*, when we first met, Bradley's passion for writing was a natural gas pocket looking for a lighter. Steady fuel supplied his daily habit of writing and posting to his blogs.

He figured there were some books in there somewhere.

He had already decided he didn't want to do what he'd been doing for all those years when he was pretending he wasn't a writer.

He was open to more, confused about much, and curious about EVERYTHING. He was making those small decisions he talks about in this book. The ones that lead you closer to places you are drawn to visit, yet haven't quite decided to live.

On #912 ESD Bradley had no idea what was coming. He hadn't gotten up going, "today is the day my life changes." However, he was the one who decided in a split second to say yes to all he'd secretly been asking for.

My guess is that when he reads this foreword for the first time he will be surprised to make the connection that his exuberant decision (as in jumping up and down on the side of the road) to blurt out the words, "Hey, give it to me. I'll take it," altered the course of his life.

As Bradley writes in *Decide*, our hearts will guide us to make decisions if we trust it. He wasn't using his thinking decision making skills when he said those words, he was deciding from a place of inner knowing. A knowing that told him very quickly and clearly, "I want that!"

And with that simple decision he got more than a Bic lighter that would quickly run out of fuel, he got a lifetime supply of fireworks! When his heart exploded with electricity, sending bolts of orange, red and yellow into his body, Bradley's writing caught fire and he's never looked back.

Decide is sort of a prequel to *Every Single Day*, which documented Bradley's challenges and successes, and how his decision to write for 30 days led to #2165 ESD and counting.

Decide will always be a work in progress. Such is the joy of technology that authors can easily update their published work as more decisions lead to more questions that lead to more answers that lead to more decisions.

It's a beautiful cycle. One that encourages curiosity, allows for more, and negates the pressure to come up with the right decision.

Decide to dive in now.

Answer one, or all, of those 71 questions for yourself. Who knows what doors will open for you?

The answers you decide are true for you, may well be different from Bradley's, and that is a very good thing.

After all, it got you to Decide.

Adwynna MacKenzie

Author of Carefree, Book 1: It Starts With Open, where you can read the rest of Bradley's #912 ESD story.

PART I
THINK

1
INTRODUCTION
THINK

"Procrastination is opportunity's assassin."

— Victor Kiam

That thing you think is going to happen might not happen. You think it will. It probably will. No, it will. But then, it might not.

"I know it will get done at some point."

But what if it never gets done?

A few days after my father's passing, I was in his office in his house. There were stacks of paper on his desk. For some reason, those stacks of paper affected me deeply.

Although my dad was gone from the physical world, those papers did not go with him. Since my dad's passing, I am happy to say that I somehow have a lighter view on what it means to leave the physical realm of life as we know it.

Now you might be scratching your head wondering how I jumped from papers on a desk to some sort of spiritual afterworld, but I'll connect the dots, I promise.

I'd like to think there is an administrative office in heaven where you sit down in a plush chair, are offered a Chai tea latte, and they tell you every checkbox, all of your to-do lists, and pretty much everything you ever needed to finish, have been completed.

Since this is heaven and I struggled to gather interview subjects for this research, we're going to have to go with hearsay.

Because if it's truly heaven and it lives up to all of the hype, then not only will your to-do lists and public tasks be completed, but even those dreams you had hidden deep in your heart are either done or, maybe even better, are now available for you to finish and you had all of the resources and all of the time and all of the energy you needed to make it happen.

Now that I have heaven covered, let's move back to the physical, alive realm of earth and life as we know it.

Those papers on the desk.

They're not going to complete themselves, on their own, without you, or by some heavenly administrative angel. Yeah, sorry about that.

In fact, as far as my dad taking care of those papers, I feel quite certain to state they will never get done.

Never

"Never" is one of those short, five letter words, that are hard for us to comprehend because our minds can't get a hold on something like infinity. Again, let's descend back to the world we know of finite time, of say for example, a lifetime, or next Thursday.

"Next Thursday" is the opposite of never. Next Thursday is a finite, defined deadline I just pulled out of thin air but here's the beauty of the next Thursday deadline: if I decide to get it done by that date, and I follow through on my decision, it will be done and the option for "never" is now off the table.

To delve into semantics for just a moment and combine it with simple mathematics, "someday" and "never" have the same numerical value in that they both equal zero, or in other words, they are valueless, they have no worth, it will never get done.

Decide

The difference between something getting done and something not getting done is extremely simple yet not necessarily always easy.

There is a distance between done and not done that either can be measured with a microscope or satellite imagery. In other words, the difference between done and not done is either so tiny we can't see it or so vast we can't see it either.

The difference between the two comes down to one simple, not always easy, action: decide.

Maybe my dad had decided to take care of one or some or all of the papers on his desk, but he just ran out of time.

Remember when I said I would connect the dots? This is that moment.

Although we have the power to make a decision today, that does not equate to accomplishing what we decide, it only means we have chosen our path and we have taken the first step.

However, let me be clear, by making a decision to go forward at least opens up the opportunity for success whereas by not deciding or, of course, deciding not to do something, the statistical probability of achieving that thing is down to a big, fat, simple to understand zero.

In simple mathematics, the difference between zero and any other number, be it one or 427, is the same.

The difference being the same as the difference between yes or no, done or not done, alive or dead.

Putting aside momentarily the angelic staff of administrative superheroes, we have one power on this earth that is potentially our greatest strength as humans.

That power is to decide.

2
OOPS, THAT'S ONE DECISION ALREADY
DIDN'T EVEN NOTICE, DID YOU?

> "The most difficult thing is the decision to act, the rest is merely tenacity. The fears are paper tigers. You can do anything you decide to do. You can act to change and control your life; and the procedure, the process is its own reward."
>
> — AMELIA EARHART

There are several arrows on the cover of this book.

On an earlier design of the cover, there were four arrows, one of the arrows was facing down or back or in reverse or returning or giving up or whatever negative label we'd like to give it.

However, and I might add this is part of the mysterious, secretive, and powerful spell that decisions have on us, because you looked at the image, the graphic, the arrows and thought about it for a split second, wondered what they meant, deciphered and translated and interpreted your own meaning of where those arrows were going and what direction they were going in, that is already a decision past zero.

Just the tiniest of thoughts, a beginning, a forming, a seed of an idea is already one step in the direction in the decision-making process.

Because you saw this book, because you even glanced at it, because your brain analyzed the arrows and thought about them, there is no turning back. Now the decision has you under its spell.

I'm trying not to say this in a threatening manner, but more of one of respect. Respect for the power of the decision. That we are conscious of the hundreds or thousands of tiny decisions that constantly alter the trajectory on a second by second, minute by minute, and day by day basis, all the time, every year, throughout our lives.

As I write this, I completely realize it may seem daunting, it may seem like a huge dark cloud weighing upon us.

But this is where we turn things around.

This is where we climb up through that huge dark cloud, scramble up through the damp cotton ball world, rise up to where things are lighter, fluffier, and drier.

We arrive at the point where we are on top of that cloud, where we use it as a trampoline but don't bounce around haphazardly like a toddler, but rather use the exponential power because as we are conscious of our thoughts, ideas, and decisions, they begin to work for us.

No longer is the weight of decisions heavy on our shoulders, but rather it becomes the spring in our step.

There is no arrow facing downward.

There is no return from this point.

You cannot unsee the image of the three arrows for they are now ingrained in your mind forever.

Having this information, knowing that there now is no way back, you tighten the laces on your shoes, you lift your chin up, and look forward towards your next decision.

3

A SMIDGEN OF A GLANCE AT THE SEED OF A THOUGHT
WELL, THAT SEEMS INSIGNIFICANT.

"Often, little situations trigger enormous reactions. Be there, present for it. Your partner will find it easier to see it in you, and you will find it easier to see it in them."

— Eckhart Tolle

A billboard. A bird. A wink from a stranger. What that woman said in the film last night. The touch of his hand on your shoulder. A book.

Something triggered the first thought. A tiny little speck of almost nothingness caused the beginning of something that sent the next thing into action which rolled into that part and finally ended up as that thing.

Can we trace it all back?

Did you move to Spain because your aunt Penelope said her cousin bought a sombrero and even though that's Mexican and not Spanish her cousin told you a story about her friend who lives in Valencia and introduced you? Then three years later you were married to the friend's accountant?

All from a sombrero?

A smidgen of a glance at the seed of a thought.

They happen all the time. Which ones stick? Which ones fizzle out? Which ones cannot be stopped even if you wanted them to?

Are they under our control? If so, how much? A little? All control? I doubt it.

How much are we involved? Is it fate or do we have a choice in the matter?

The sombrero? Seriously?

Watch out for what triggers the slightest trajectory change in your decision-making process.

Listen to aunt Penelope.

You never know where things might lead.

4

NOT SIMPLE AND NOT EASY
LET'S MAKE IT ALL REALLY COMPLICATED

"Life is really simple, but we insist on making it complicated."

— Confucius

*J*ust in case things went too quickly for you back in the introduction, let's make sure we've checked all of the boxes to get rolling.

1. Not Simple
2. Not Easy

This is a good place to start so it will get better as we go along.

Not Simple

We have a lot to cover in this book. Tons. Maybe we should make it a 3-volume set. Let's call it Complex. Complicated. Rocket Science.

We might need a follow-up workshop (complete with really long workbook) to run through all of the steps. Maybe we need an app, too. Apps are great. Yes, we need more apps.

OK, sorry. Let me get back to not simple.

This is a big decision we're up against. We're up against the decision to, well, make more decisions.

"Because it's difficult, it must be complex."

— Someone Probably Said

Let's go with weight loss. Simple, right? Lose weight!

Slow down there, Pendergrass. We need to learn about nutrition and our diet, do tests to test our sugar levels and how many carbs we should balance with our proteins. What are proteins, anyway? Let's take a course at the local college. That should take a semester. Then we'll start on the diet.

Complicated.

Good. Have we covered that well enough? Let's move on to even worse things.

Not Easy

We just learned we have loads to do and it's going to take a long time. That can't be fun. That can't be easy. Let's make sure we have it all lined up. I smell a numbered list coming ...

1. **Checkboxes:** we're going to need lots of lists to check off what we're doing. It might help tone down the Not Simple a little if we have multiple, categorized, color-coded lists.
2. **Time:** did you sign up for the course on nutrition yet? I'm not even sure they're open for enrollment until the next semester.
3. **Peers:** tell our friends and family or not tell our friends and family? If we do we'll have some accountability. That could get ugly. If we keep it to ourselves and then only go public when we've made some progress we'll be a success story and it will be easier to talk about.

4. **Mindset:** we can't forget that we need to make this Not Easy so we're convinced it will work. If it were too simple and too easy, it certainly wouldn't work. I mean, right? Mindset shift: this is Not Easy.

That seems complicated enough.
Action Steps

1. Get going on the list building.
2. Buy colored pencils. Or maybe pens. Whatever is erasable.
3. Sign up for college course on nutrition.
4. Tell friends. Or don't.
5. Change my mindset to make sure I know it's going to be Not Simple and Not Easy.

No, the Real Action Steps

1. Don't do any of the above action steps.
2. Keep reading.
3. Get a cup of tea or coffee.

We'll get past this.

5
WHAT WAS THAT TINGLE IN THE HAIRS ON THE BACK OF YOUR NECK?
IT MIGHT BE THE SOMBRERO

"If I don't get the goose-bump factor when I'm reading it then I can't do it."

— RUSSELL CROWE

Just as you're doubting the whole sombrero escapade, the hairs on the back of your neck start to tingle.

I could throw loads of science your way backing up the numbers behind the decision-making trajectory and possibly wow you with all kinds of theories and books and research.

Or the hairs on the back of your neck could stand up.

I'm all for science. I'm a numbers guy, a math lover, a guy who often reads the manual.

But then comes along gut feeling.

When you just know. Or at least it feels like something is right (or wrong). It's not provable, you can't necessarily share the why or what or how, but it's just there.

I say this way too often in my books, but you can skip the rest of the chapters and go with this one if you'd like. That gut feeling? Those hairs on your neck? Goosebumps?

To me, those are the indicators that defy logic. The telltale signs of something larger at play.

I'm not saying you have to believe me. I'm only asking that you keep an open mind.

The next time you have that feeling—and you know what it is, however it comes your way—take note of it.

Take a moment and think about whatever it was that you just did that caused something in your body to do something.

Our own power of thought is something many of us underestimate or even take for granted. All we did was create a thought and it caused a physical reaction in our physical body.

When else does that happen?

If we're scared, we might flinch. If we're sad, we might cry.

But here, something is triggered and it's causing a physical reaction. Are they not the same thing?

The power of our own thoughts is something we can use to our advantage.

Take that confidence, that feeling of goodness and hold onto it because we're about to head into the section of the book called doubt.

PART II
DOUBT

INTRODUCTION
DOUBT

> "Procrastination is one of the most common and deadliest of diseases and its toll on success and happiness is heavy."
>
> — Wayne Gretzky

I realize we just finished the section that ended with happy places like sombreros and hairs tingling on your neck. I daresay that this section titled "Doubt" is optional, but I'm going to say it anyway. It's optional.

"But I like doubt! Doubt gives me freedom from deciding and doesn't force me to move forward! It's a cozy, friendly place where I can hang out forever!"

> — Bradley Charbonneau (not the author of this book, but another Bradley clearly)

I mostly want to give you the out, the chance, the right to make doubt optional. Let me put it this way: I used to believe doubt wasn't optional. In fact, it was a clear link in the chain of the whole, really long, cumbersome process.

Let me skip ahead a few chapters: it's optional.

We don't need to doubt.

Sure, we can analyze and weigh the pros and cons, but the doubt I'm referring to is more of the sombrero and neck hair variety. It's the kind we don't need to, well, doubt.

With that, if you'd like to trudge along knee-deep in the morass of swampy doubt, let's get started.

7

THE SCHOOL UNIFORM AND UNLEASHING MASSIVE BRAIN POWER
LET'S SEE, HOW ABOUT THE WHITE BUTTON DOWN AND THE KHAKI PANTS TODAY?

"Creativity is piercing the mundane to find the marvelous."

— Bill Moyers

Unless you're a kid and go to a school where they require you to wear the same exact uniform to school every single day, you have a decision to make on a morning-by-morning basis.

Those kids, however much they dislike the white polo shirt and khaki pants for the boys and a pleated long skirt for the girls, have one pretty big decision less to make every morning.

They don't even think about it anymore.

It's now ingrained in them to not make a decision because that decision was made for them and will be made for them as long as they're at that school.

Each morning there is free space in their brains for different, better, hopefully bigger decisions.

That free space will make those other decisions easier.

Let's do a little math.

1. School uniform

2. Breakfast
3. Brain power jet fuel

1 + 2 < 3

One plus two is less than three.

Did you catch that little bonus in there? Because no energy was expended on #1 and there's left over energy for #2, there is even more energy left for the post-#2 decisions of the day.

#1 is done

#2 is easier

#3 is extra brain power

Anything beyond #2 (e.g. #3, #4, #5, etc.) is better, easier, and double bonus brownie points: even *stronger* each day.

As we make decisions, even the smallest of them, our brain gets better at it. It's a muscle. If we exercise it, it can get stronger.

It also realizes very soon when it doesn't have to make the #1 decision and can more quickly get to #2.

TIP: What could we do for the #2 decision of the day to make that a non-decision as well (if applicable). Pretty soon our breakfast-choice decision-making will be something measured in nanoseconds.

Can you see where this is going?

After breakfast you'll be solving the economic crisis in Greece. By lunch, you'll have so much extra brain power you'll be hot on the trail of a new cure for cancer.

As your decision-making expertise grows, even the bigger decisions will become easier.

Ah, the day when you look back and sigh at the energy and neurons you spent agonizing over the beige socks or the brown socks. How many hours of your life did you scuttle away?

If the school uniform doesn't do it for you, let's list just a few that might get your attention:

1. Lose weight
2. Stop smoking
3. Quit job

Doubtful? We are still in the section of this book called "Doubt," after all.

If every single morning, you didn't have to decide whether or not you were going to continue on your weight loss regimen, you would have that much more room in your mind to, for example, think about new ways to make it happen faster.

Fashion note: this is not to say that wearing the same thing for the rest of your life is a good idea. In fact, as we'll dig into later, there are some decisions on a regular basis that are fun--or can turn into fun as we get better at making decisions in general.

8

LET'S DECIDE THIS BETTER TOGETHER
ASK ME WHAT I THINK YOU SHOULD DO

"Every question is a hypothetical question for everyone but the person who asks it."

— Dan Savage

*C*ompared to the relatively simple example of the school uniform, many decisions are not solely ours to make.

This might fall into the topic of another one-word verb book of mine, Ask, but let's for a minute think about those decisions that are possibly out of your own decision-making power.

When you're in doubt and you'd like the feedback from others, be selective in where you seek that help.

There's really only one rule when asking others about your decision:

Do they have your best interest at heart?

I love the oxygen mask in the airplane metaphor. Yep, you want to save your child next to you when there's no oxygen in the plane.

The quick and doubtful decision might be to get her the oxygen.

But then you die.

Then, well, there are about a zillion circumstances here at play in my imaginary (and terribly distressing!) example, but let's go with it as we've come this far.

But the longer-term decision is for you to take the oxygen first. Then you can:

- Care for yourself.
- Better care for the child.
- Both survive.

I'm all about collaboration and cooperation, but is asking others the best route? Be selective, be cautious, gauge whether or not your best interest is in their heart.

Ideally, you'll be better together.

9

THE TINY LITTLE SECRET OF THE TIPPING POINT

A LITTLE MORE, A LITTLE LESS.

"I don't think anyone, until their soul leaves their body, is past the point of no return."

— Tom Hiddleston

There's a fear among non-decision makers that a tipping point comes along that's so big it might knock us over.

The secret of the tipping point is that we are constantly at a point of tipping.

Sure, there are bigger decisions and smaller ones, medium-sized ones and a few doozies.

But each point is a tipping point.

Each point leads to the next one and that then is the next tipping point. Which, guess what? Leads to the next one.

The trick, the art, the secret of these tipping points is to keep them small, to keep them active, and to be tipping them all the time so we become used to them and they're no longer big and scary.

More fulfilled, less fulfilled. More meaning, flow, satisfaction--or less.

If each so-called tipping point, or let's tone it down a little and pull out all of the pomp and circumstance around the words, each *decision* is just a question of more fulfilled or less fulfilled, more bliss or less bliss, more gut feeling or less gut feeling, then it's easier to make that decision.

It should--and will--become as easy as a flowing river or a stick floating in that river that goes where the current is the strongest.

It's pulled a little this way, it's pushed a little that way. But it's not using any of its own energy, it's just, dare I use the pun, going with the flow.

Which is, of course, exactly the point.

As we tip, as we knock over each point along the way, just like a runner who is in shape and runs at least a little bit every day, the medium runs are easier. Even the marathon is something they're prepared for. Yes, it's a big deal, but they are more ready for it, it's not a surprise, in fact, it's a welcome challenge.

As we become more experienced with tipping, we even look forward to it as we know with each tip the next one will be that much easier.

PART III

DECIDE

INTRODUCTION
DECIDE

"Because there is a law such as gravity, the universe can and will create itself from nothing."

— STEPHEN HAWKING

W e're at the mountain peak.
We made it.
But now what?
Go back from where we came? Turn left? Turn right?
Or continue what we started?
We've come this far. It's time to go through with it.
Let's say it's winter and we have a snowball in our hands. We're at the top of the mountain. We can walk it down and hold it in our hands back the way we came. Maybe toss it off to the left or right.
Or send it on its way straight ahead. Let it head down the hill. Gain momentum. Build up speed. Get bigger and bigger.
Soon, there will be no stopping it.
Because we have reached the midpoint of this book and we have decided.

There's no turning back now.

OK, fine, you can turn back. You can stop reading, I suppose. But then I should write a follow-up book called, "Undecided: It was my choice. I didn't do it."

Let's head to the field of dreams.

11
DECIDE AND PEOPLE WILL COME
IF YOU DON'T, THEY WON'T

"People will come, Ray. People will most definitely come."

— James Earl Jones as Terence Mann (from Field of Dreams)

Math. I have to go back to math.

If my 14-year-old son ever reads this, he'll cringe at the thought of my bringing up math yet again in my work.

Maybe if he reads a little later, like when he's 34, he'll understand that math can be the great explainer.

Zero.

It doesn't really exist. It's nothing. It's not yet something.

The quote above is from the film Field of Dreams and the main character is debating creating a baseball field in the middle of a cornfield in Iowa.

One.

One exists. It's a real number. It's just one more than zero, but remember, zero doesn't exist.

If he doesn't build the baseball diamond, by definition, no one will come, no one will visit it because it doesn't exist.

If he does build it at least there's a chance people will come.

Now Terence Mann seems pretty convinced people will come. But then again, they're talking about baseball and cornfields and Iowa.

In this book, we're talking about your decisions, your plans, your dreams, your life.

If you decide, will they come?

In case that little math above didn't put you on the edge of your seat just begging for more numbers, here's the statistical probability of something happening if you do not decide:

Zero.

We're back to zero. Zero chance, zero nothing, zero nada.

If you decide, will they come?

There's no guarantee, but now there's a chance.

Here's how I see it. If you decide, they will be *swayed*.

They will respect your decision (whether they admit it openly or not for whatever reasons).

If you stick with your decision, at some point, they have to respect that you made the decision and stuck with it.

If you succeed in making the decision and then sticking with the decision and then following through and succeeding (however success might be interpreted), in my humble opinion, people will respect that.

Am I just seeking respect?

Yes.

But not from others. I care less about what they think—although I do care.

No, I'm seeking *self-respect*.

When I make the decision and keep it and follow through and make it happen, I have self-respect.

No one can take that from me. Ever. It's mine and I'm not giving it up. It's tight in my fist and no one, no one can rip it out of my fingers.

It's mine.

It's yours.
Keep it.
Decide.

12

SIMPLE BUT NOT EASY
WE'RE ALMOST THERE

"A song that sounds simple is just not that easy to write. One of the objectives of this record was to try and write melodies that continue to resonate."

— Sheryl Crow

There was a radio show called Car Talk where two guys (Click and Clack, the Tappet Brothers) talked about car repair.

I know, sounds really boring (unless you're really into car repair). But the guys were hilarious. People flocked to the show even if they cared nothing for cars.

They had off-the-wall solutions for most things (e.g. don't replace the car, replace your husband) and laughed throughout most of the program.

I searched and couldn't find an exact quote, but they had an episode where they talked about how simple it was to replace a car engine. Here are the steps. I remember them clearly because they were so simple.

1. Remove old engine.
2. Put in new engine.

That was it.
Simple, but not easy.
Which, of course, was their point—and their joke.
The answers are often simple. The execution can be the hard part.
Let's take a perennial favorite: weight loss.

1. Simple: eat less (and better). Move (exercise) more.
2. Not Easy: do that.

We all know how simple it is, but we want to make it not easy so we can:

1. Procrastinate.
2. Buy books and courses and gym memberships.
3. Not really do it at all.
4. Talk about how much we want to do it.
5. Buy another book.
6. Join another group.
7. Make friends who also don't do it–but would all really, really like to.
8. Sulk.
9. Eat chips.
10. Start this list over at #1.

See how complicated that all got? Whew. I need a break.
For now, halfway through this book, we're shooting for simple.
We'll deal with *easy* later.
For the record, I'm also "trying to lose weight" and am currently un-happily repeating step #3 with a healthy dose of #9.
But as Yoda said, "There is no try."
We'll get to that later, too.

13

RELIEF

THE FEELING WHEN IT CLICKS

"Effort only fully releases its reward after a person refuses to quit."

— Napoleon Hill

There's a point in decision making, probably quite a bit like reaching the summit of a mountain on a bicycle, when you feel relief. If the word relief doesn't quite do it for you, let's try:

- release
- satisfaction
- alleviation
- deliverance
- happiness

Everything from letting go to joy. There are standard lines we hear when you feel relief. Any of these strike a chord?

- I'm so glad that's over!
- I can't believe that was all there was to it.
- Whew. I never thought I'd get there.

- I did it. I actually did it.

These are statements of relief. This is what happens when you decide.

People ask all the time, "But how do I know when I've made the right decision?" Usually my answer is "You'll just know." or maybe "You'll feel it."

But the word relief is easier to swallow, to comprehend, to really feel. People know the feeling of relief.

- You just avoided a car wreck.
- You finally got that project done by the deadline.
- Your spouse got the numbers back from the doctor.

But relief can be achieved, reached, influenced.

It doesn't only have to be something we receive or react to. It can be something we can proactively make happen.

Through deciding, through making a decision, we can build it to the point where we feel relief because we made that decision. In fact, that's the trick, that's the rub, that's the big secret: we know we have made the right decision when we feel that relief.

It's a gut feeling, a feeling thing.

It's not science, but more of an art. I know you don't want to hear it, but you'll just know.

Once you get better at building small levels of relief, you'll improve at sensing when you feel that relief, how much of it, the level of importance, and how to then take it even to the next level.

When things get really, really interesting.

PART IV

FLOW

INTRODUCTION
FLOW

"I just go with the flow, I follow the yellow brick road. I don't know where it's going to lead me, but I follow it."

— GRACE JONES

We're heading down the mountain. The snowball is building in speed and size. We have momentum. Not only is it difficult to turn back, we no longer want to.

We've made the decision.

Now it's time to reap the glory.

We just need to keep it going. Stick with it. Persevere. Be patient.

If others are falling away around you, it's OK. In fact, it might even be seen as a good sign: you're on your path anyway, not theirs.

Here we go.

Hold on.

15

DECISIONS BEGET DECISIONS
SHE DID THAT SO WE DID THIS WHICH LED TO THEM MAKING THAT HAPPEN

> "The process of writing is like creating a game of dominoes: The first domino creates the second incident, and so forth until the end."
>
> — Asghar Farhadi

My mom moved. After 49 years in the same house. I went out there and spent two weeks, 8-10 hours per day, sifting through 49 years of stuff.

beget: to cause; produce as an effect

We're renovating our house here in The Netherlands. We have to move out for 10 weeks. We're in a little "vacation house" in this "vacation park" in the woods where City Folk come to get away from it all. It's cute, it's quiet, it's small. From the moving truck that went to my wife's mom's cellar, we took only suitcases and a few things. Even too many small few things.

Last week the papers were signed and we sold an investment property we had in California. A few years ago, it would have been a huge deal, a monumental decision, but we now just did it.

Decisions Beget Decisions

My mom decided to move. We decided to renovate. We decided to sell our house.

They influence each other. Each one made the next one easier. Note that they weren't even our own decisions, we were influenced, intrigued, and inspired by the decisions of others.

My sister now said that she ...

See how it works?

Just as we are influenced by actions, behaviors, thoughts, moods or others (and ourselves), we are influenced by the decisions and the decision-making power of others.

We can get better at making decisions. We will learn that not making a decision is actually a decision. That stalling, whining, procrastinating is really just costing us time, energy, and probably money.

Start with small ones. Work up to bigger ones. Talk to people who made the big ones. Ask them about them. How did it make them feel? What were the pros and cons? How could you learn from their decisions to make your own? How can we learn from our own decisions--and lack thereof--to make better ones from here on out?

It's like a muscle and we can work it, use it, train it, and get smarter about it.

16

THE BIG DECISIONS WILL HELP GUIDE THE SMALLER DECISIONS

THE RIVER WILL FIND A WAY

> "But the rule seems to be that the bigger and more life-changing the decision, the less it will seem like a decision at all."
>
> — Hugh Mackay

Throughout this book, we've hopefully hammered home how important the smaller decisions are. Make lots of little decisions on a regular basis (pretty much all the time) and the bigger ones will be easier, more clear, and even light and fun.

But what about those big ones?

The career change, the move cities or countries, the have kids or not? They exist, we can't deny them. Those decisions have to be made at some point. Yes, it's true, they are easier as the smaller ones are made.

I hope it hasn't felt as if I've been hiding the big ones and in anticipation it's been a worry along the way when we're going to be dealing with them. In other words, sure, you're running around the block every day, but when are you really going to tackle the marathon?

Let's let the cat out of the bag: we need to make the big decisions, too.

Here's the exciting news: when you make the big ones, the smaller ones become even easier. Yes, we've discussed how easy the small ones can be, but when you make the big ones, the smaller ones are dessert, fun, light, and like popping a bonbon in your mouth--pure delight.

Here's the scary news: yes, we have to make them.

How to prepare for them? How to actually make them happen? How to not mess up the big one so the little ones are not messed up too?

Practice.

Build up to them. Work on the small ones, then some medium ones, then the big ones will be easier.

Let's go back to our friend the river. As the tributaries lead into the main flow, the big river, it becomes more powerful. The direction of that big river becomes easier as it's flowing faster and stronger. It arrives at the big rocks, maybe even the mountain and it might plow straight into it. Maybe the mountain breaks apart under the pressure. Maybe the river goes left. Maybe it goes right.

It's going to go where the resistance is the least.

This doesn't mean it's easiest path and not the right path. It's the path, at least in the river example, where the resistance to holding back is the least strong.

In our human being example, with our now-more-experienced-decision-making minds, it's the path that feels right, that's natural, that causes the least friction, that our gut tells us is right, that our experience in decision making points us towards.

You can't decide whether or not to upgrade your house alarm system.

Or, let's take a few more from real life:

1. Do you fix the hole in the floor in the office?

2. What to do with that old (but beautiful) Chinese chest?
3. Renew the expensive cable bill?
4. Finally replace that microwave?
5. Stocks or real estate?

These are real decisions. Many of them aren't that big, but when they're in front of you (sort of like the guy with the knife in the alley, even though, in hindsight, he was short and possibly blind and potentially asleep ...), they were Big Decisions when you were trying to make them.

Which brings us to subjective and objective decision making.

With the six decisions to be made above (including the alarm system), what if they could all be answered, solved, just plain made to vanish with a single swoosh of the magic wand?

What if you just **Know What You Need to Do**? Just all of the sudden? As if a little fairy on your shoulder told you?

Here's how.

Think bigger. Think higher. Above, beyond, longer term.

However you want to see it.

Here's what happened.

A certain someone had all of the above decisions to make. They weren't weighing down her daily life, but they were still on her mind. Occasionally, they were annoying. It would have been nice if they went away.

Then one day, possibly (no, probably) partly related to those decisions weighing down on her for weeks (if not months or years), she had a moment of clarity that would demote all of those decisions (and many, many more) from primary to secondary.

She decided it was time to move.

Move houses. Move out from where the hole in the office was. Move to a place where the Chinese chest (yes, she'd had it in the family for decades) had no place. Where cable TV was included. An alarm system built in. A microwave built after 1974 was already in the kitchen.

No longer were these decisions even on the table. They were gone. They were answered. They vanished into thin air. Just like that.

Because she thought bigger and made a larger, much more important decision.

As if the previously large decisions were buoys floating in the ocean (hard to collect, bobbing up and down, but clearly visible) and the big, new decision was the fishing boat that came through and just swept all of the buoys up and away.

Just like that, all of those decisions that used to weigh you down were now done. Answered.

Like magic.

17

WHEN YOU CHANGE YOUR MIND, YOU CHANGE YOUR MIND
NEURONS AND STUFF

"In the brain, you have connections between the neurons called synapses, and they can change. All your knowledge is stored in those synapses."

— Geoffrey Hinton

It's not just a thought, matter changes form when you make a decision.

In case my witty play on words didn't make complete sense, let me explain what I'm getting at:

When you (1) change your mind, that is, when you make a decision, you (2) change your mind, that is, you alter the chemistry of your brain.

There are of course varying levels of how much happens, but it happens. Even when you're driving and you decide to go left instead of right, there is so much activity in your brain and part of it sticks.

If something changes in your brain with such a simple decision, can you imagine how much transforms when you make a big decision?

Decisions--and changes in brain neurons--are relative and subjective.

In other words, what might seem a small decision to some (your decision to stop eating sugar for a month) is huge to others. But what matters most is how much it matters to you, how much it changes how your neurons are firing, what is connecting with what in your brain, what sticks, and what gets altered.

When you make a decision, you change your mind, you alter your brain.

Are you ready to change your mind? Think it wasn't possible? Change your mind, change your brain, alter your neurons.

- Change more of them.
- Do it on a regular basis.
- Get better at it.
- Get in "decision making" shape where it becomes easier and easier to make them.
- Get stronger with them.
- Make bigger ones.
- Change your mind.
- Change your brain.
- Change your habits.
- Change your life.

Oh, one more thing.

It works both ways.

Notice I haven't talked about success or better or even worse. Because it can go both ways. You can make more bad decisions. You can alter your mind for the worse just as easily as for the better.

See how you have the power? See how there's risk, danger, but also opportunity?

Want to know the best part?

It's up to you.

Are you going to change your mind today?
Here's my bet: having read this today, you already have.

PART V
PLAY

INTRODUCTION
PLAY

"Play is often talked about as if it were a relief from serious learning. But for children play is serious learning. Play is really the work of childhood."

— Fred Rogers

*I*f you thought flow was fun, this is going to be an extra special treat.

There comes a time when you've done something for a while when you are convinced so clearly and purely that you no longer remember or recognize (or maybe it's just that you no longer care) about how you started or where you began.

We're deep in flow. We have momentum, confidence, and passion. We have long since made our decision.

Now we get to the unexpected benefits that come with decision making.

Play.

19

GIVE A VOICE TO YOUR TRUTH AND A TRUTH TO YOUR VOICE
IT'S TIME TO SPEAK UP

"There is but one cause of human failure. And that is man's lack of faith in his true Self."

— WILLIAM JAMES

Unblock the dam and let the river flow as it was meant to.
We all have an inner voice or we can call it our subconscious self or it's actually fine to call it or relate to it however you want. But I think something is there, something is in there and when we are connected with it, when we are aligned with it, following it, allowing ourselves to be pulled by it, then things are easier, more meaningful, and, dare I say, effortless.

Not just effortless in that it doesn't cost us any energy, but it's actually on the other side of the neutral line from negative--it's positive. It provides energy.

Whereas when we fight it, when we push back, when we deny and avoid and pretend it isn't there, maybe never was there--when we know full well it is there, was there, and will continue to be there--we're just delaying the pain, the regret, the, dare I say, the lie.

Maybe I'm wrong.

Do you remember in school when we learned about water and how it will find a way? It will get through the mountain or around it or under it. It might build up and finally burst in a flood. Or it will trickle through the soil and create underground rivers and caverns. It's not in any big hurry. It will get there. It's also fine to wait. It will prevail.

It can also take on other forms. It can freeze while inside of a rock and break that formidable foe slowly and surely. Or it might evaporate and go above the mountain only to rain down on the other side.

See how it's not going to give up? It's going to get there. No matter what.

This is how I see our truth.

If the word truth isn't doing it for you, let's think of a few other ways to say it:

- Your true self
- Who you really are
- Who you know you are but don't want to admit
- Your passion (kinda cheesy, I admit)
- Your love
- Your truth

By giving a voice to your truth, you'll be admitting, accepting, and, ideally, embracing that this voice is yours.

How do you know what your truth is? It's easy. In fact, it's not just easy to figure out, the "easy" is part of the answer, part of the roadmap to help find it.

What comes easily to you?

What, like the water, won't (let you) give up?

What gives you satisfaction?

What, when you're not doing it or being it, makes you feel unsatisfied?

Like the water, it won't go away. Ever. It might change forms (ice, steam) but it's still there.

My thinking is then to decide to give into it, to allow it, to surrender to it, to accept it, to embrace it even.

It's a conscious decision. Your truth is there, you probably know what it is. But to decide to allow it is a moment in your life when things, most things, maybe all things, will then be set free.

They will flow.

They will find their way.

More easily.

Like the river.

When you decide to give a voice to your truth.

20

WHY DON'T THEY TEACH THIS IN SCHOOL? OR ANYWHERE?

OR MAYBE I JUST MISSED THAT DAY

"You gain strength, courage, and confidence by every experience in which you really stop to look fear in the face. You are able to say to yourself, 'I lived through this horror. I can take the next thing that comes along.'"

— Eleanor Roosevelt

Maybe because I'm no longer 17 or 23 or one of those times in your life when you're pretty sure you know everything, don't need anyone to teach you anything else, and wonder why the world doesn't know what you know, but now I feel, again, like I'm 23.

Like I have the answers—or at least some of them.

As I continue to do, to write, to experience, to weigh, to ask, to answer, and to discover, I find that we can have our cake and eat it too.

We might have to bake it. It might be undercooked. The frosting might be frumpy or runny but we can have our cake and eat it too.

I suppose if I knew what I knew now when I was 17 or 23 (or 33 ...), I wouldn't be right for that age.

Do we learn what we need to learn when we need to learn it? When the time is right? When it's appropriate?

I don't believe in holding back knowledge. I want to share everything I know if it can make someone's life better or easier or more of whatever it is they're after.

Maybe they don't teach decision making in school. But if you've learned anything about it in this book, please pass it along to someone who's 17 or 23 or at least ... thinks they are.

21

WHEN ARE DECISIONS TRIGGERED IN THE SUBCONSCIOUS MINDS OF CHILDREN?

MEMORIES WITH EMOTION

"A strong emotion, especially if experienced for the first time, leaves a vivid memory of the scene where it occurred."

— ALGERNON BLACKWOOD

The good news and the bad news: they're triggered all the time.

As an adult, I'm very conscious of the fact that memories are being recorded (and tiny decisions being made) all the time in my kids--and all kids ... and all people for that matter.

The thing is: you don't know which ones are going to stick.

Or do you?

The memories with emotion are the ones that are going to stick.

You can go to a lot of trouble to make it all a big deal to try to force the memory, that important moment, but the truth is, it's going to be what it's going to be. But can we force in some emotion so it will stick?

We can try.

As much as I think it'd be wonderful if my son went to the University of Groningen, I have little influence as to what will happen in his future. Well, I have some influence, but it's a bit like herding jellyfish: you don't want to touch them and they're just so squishy (not to mention they sting and it hurts like hell).

But some things can stick more than others.

We visited the Dutch city of Groningen for a few days and the impressions of the student town might stick in my son's mind forever.

He might remember the thump-your-heart-bass-beat of the bouncing student float. Whereas I might remember the Harry Potter-esque university building.

Then again, it might be reversed.

Who knows.

That's the beauty of the triggering of the decision-making process. We can think we have some influence, but it might go completely in another direction.

The good news? That's actually good news. If we could predict everything, what fun would that be?

22

SIMPLE AND EASY
IT'S POSSIBLE

"Happiness does not come from doing easy work but from the afterglow of satisfaction that comes after the achievement of a difficult task that demanded our best."

— THEODORE ISAAC RUBIN

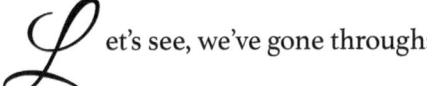et's see, we've gone through:

- Not Simple and Not Easy
- Simple but Not Easy

and now we come to Simple and Easy. Could it be possible that something is both simple and easy? Wouldn't that be too good to be true?

Doesn't our hard-working upbringing tell us that it takes hard work, perseverance, and patience to get what really matters in life?

What if it weren't true?

Or at least partly untrue? Or at least a sliver of the alternative of it was possible?

Once we make the decision, the real one we're going to stick with. The one that gives us the goosebumps or makes the hairs stand up on our neck. We'll know there's no turning back.

The best way I can describe it is as a snowball.

It's simple and easy.

23

SNOWBALL

YOU MIGHT WANT TO GET OUT OF THE WAY

"People often say motivation doesn't last. Well, neither does bathing. That's why we recommend it daily."

— Zig Ziglar

The "snowball effect" is what I'm going to end with. It's so appropriate on so many levels I just can't not do it.

It's simple.

It's easy.

Here's what Wikipedia has to say:

"Metaphorically, a snowball effect is a process that starts from an initial state of small significance and **builds upon itself,** becoming larger (graver, more serious), and also perhaps potentially dangerous or disastrous (a vicious circle), though it might be beneficial instead (a virtuous circle). This is a cliché in cartoons and modern theatrics and it is also used in psychology.

The common analogy is with the rolling of a snowball down a snow-covered hillside. As it rolls the ball will pick up more snow, gaining more mass and surface area, and picking up even more snow and **momentum** as it rolls along."

When you make the decision to do something, when you decide there will not be any turning back, when you know, you just know, that this is what you'll be doing for the foreseeable future, then the snowball is all you need.

Sure, you might think, "It's just frozen water. How powerful could that be?"

But it's growing, it's rolling, it's faster and getting faster. It has gravity on its side. It has momentum. It has nothing in its way except maybe the other side of the valley.

Although we have covered many aspects of decisions and the decision-making process in this book, this is the one that's most exciting.

Like a little snowball at the top of a mountain, at first it seems so innocent, so playful, so childlike.

But as it rolls down the hill and gains speed and size and weight, you quickly know there is no stopping it.

This is partly why I see this book, Decide, as the prequel to my Every Single Day book.

You need to make the snowball at the top of the hill. You need to **decide** to roll it down the mountain.

The every single day element is the rolling, the unstoppable force that the decision becomes.

Gravity. Momentum. Passion. Gut feeling. Know. Certain. Power. Ease. Play.

Snowball.

PART VI
POSTSCRIPT

24

DECIDE U.
SEE YOU IN CLASS

"When it all boils down, it's about embracing each others' stories and maybe even finding that synergy to collaborate for the common good."

— Dhani Jones

*B*ooks are awesome. Read them, cherish them, think about them, refer to them, highlight things, and ... then what?

Put it on the shelf or let it drift away in the digital wasteland in the vast warehouse of your e-reader.

What if there were a place we could connect? Just a little more? Share ideas, work together, make this whole thing even better?

I've created a companion website to accompany this book where I want to share more about the decision-making process. Where we can watch videos from experts in the field. Where we can communicate with each other, ask questions, or just hang out in the back of class and listen and take notes.

In any case, a place beyond the book. Introducing:

Decide U.

To keep out the riffraff who just happen to be walking by the campus and want to come in for the lunch buffet, I'm putting a price tag on it. But as a reader of this book, we're going to waive all of that financial nonsense and let you in with a secret hall pass.

When you visit the link below to sign up, you'll be given the option of putting in a coupon code.

The coupon code below will make the price free, zero, no dollars, no Euros, no nada.

Please don't share this code with anyone who hasn't read the book as I'd like to remain a close knit group of deciders.

The coupon code is: SNOWBALL

The link to the workshop is:

decide.repossible.com

See you on campus.

25

EVERY SINGLE DAY
IT STARTS WITH THE FIRST DAY

"A dream becomes a goal when action is taken toward its achievement."

— Bo Bennett

*A*ll ready to go and don't know quite where to start? Writerly chap that I am, I suggest writing every day. It's therapeutic, meditative, and usually surprising.

I started writing because I was challenged to do so. I wasn't sure where I was heading.

Now I know.

Dare to take a first step? Or 10?

Write Every Day for 10 Days

Writing prompts, pretty pictures, directly into your email inbox. It's just 10 Days! Easy peasy, right? Spoiler alert: it might lead to more days than 10.

Head over to:

10days.repossible.com
and sign up for free.

DID ANY PART OF THIS BOOK HELP YOU IN ANY WAY?

You can make a huge difference in the life of someone else. Reviews are the most powerful element when it comes to building attention for my books.

If this book, if even one chapter, helped you in any way, please remember that a simple, honest note from you about how this book helped you in a public review on the website where you bought this book, might mean that **this book will get into the hands of those who will also benefit from it.**

I would be very grateful if you could spend just a few minutes leaving a review.

It doesn't need to be long, maybe just highlight one tiny thing where it resonated with you.

Maybe the potential reader will resonate with *you*.

Thank you very much.

Bradley Charbonneau

RELATIONSHIP

Building a relationship with my readers is one of the best things about writing.

I occasionally send an email with details about **new books, sneak peeks** into Works In Progress, early bird **deals**, as well as exclusive, **Readers Only insights** into the writing and publishing process.

If you'd like to sign up to be on my Readers Only mailing list, just click on this link and let me know which email to send to. Thank you!

bradleycharbonneau.com/subscribe/

ABOUT THE AUTHOR

Bradley Charbonneau decided to become a writer when he wrote his first letter home when living abroad in France during university.

He used that thin airmail paper that's light blue and you can't read very well if you write on both sides.

But if you're paying by the gram and you suddenly have lots to write about because you find that life becomes more alive when you put it onto paper, then you use both sides.

Then that "reality" thing got in the way for many years. That whole job and house and kids and mortgages thing. So annoying. He didn't write much.

Life wasn't quite as alive.

But he decided again when someone pushed him, challenged him to start writing again.

Since that day, he hasn't stopped.

Nowadays, all he really wants to do is tell stories, travel with his wife to oddball destinations by rickety transport, shoot baskets with his boys, try to perfect the burrito outside of California, and whisper the secrets of freedom and deep joy to whomever is within earshot and shares even the slightest inkling of curiosity.

He currently lives in a little town outside of Utrecht in The Netherlands with his wife Saskia, famous two young boys of "The Adventures of Li & Lu" fame, and their at-least-as-famous dog Pepper.

This is Bradley's twelfth book.

It is far, far, far from his last.

Find, ask, discuss, and play at:
bradleycharbonneau.com

facebook.com/bradley.charbonneau.author
twitter.com/brathocha
instagram.com/brathocha

THE END
NO, REALLY, THIS IS IT.

Thank you for reading "Decide."
It's time to decide to make this book done. The question might be for you (and for me):
Now what?
I'd love to hear what's next for you.

1. How did this book help you move forward?
2. Do you feel more in control of your decision-making process?
3. Is your life lighter?

We'll never be done making decisions, but each one is a small victory. Congratulations on making this one to finish this book.
Thank you, thank you, thank you for reading.
Sincerely,
Bradley
Driebergen, The Netherlands

ALSO BY BRADLEY CHARBONNEAU

Most of my books are also available as audiobooks (which I giddily narrate). Search for my name at your favorite audiobook distributor, slip on your headphones, and let me take you away.

Repossible

Repossible

Every Single Day (+ Playbook)

Ask

Dare

Create

Decide

Meditate

Spark

Surrender

Play

Celebrate

Evaluate

Elevate

Frequency

Every Single Day

Every Single Day Playbook

Every Single Day Kids

Every Single Day Teens (I want to write this one because I want to read this one...)

Every Single Day Parents

Charlie Holiday

Now Is Your Chance (1)

Second Chance (2)

Chance of a Lifetime (3)

For Creatives

Audio for Authors

Meditation for Creatives (2020)

Shorts

Secret Bus to Paradise

Where I (Already) Am

Pass the Sour Cream

A Trip to Hel

Drive-By Dropping

Li & Lu

The Secret of Kite Hill (1)

The Secret of Markree Castle (2)

The Key to Markree Castle (3)

The Gift of Markree Castle (4)

Driehoek (5)

Really Old ...

urban travel guide SAN FRANCISCO

REPOSSIBLE BOOK 7

MEDITATE

CLOSE YOUR EYES TO SEE, DISCOVER YOUR TRUE CREATIVE GREATNESS, AND MAKE FRIENDS WITH YOUR POWERFUL FUTURE SELF

BRADLEY CHARBONNEAU

PRAISE FOR EVERY SINGLE DAY
A QUICK SELECTION OF BOOK REVIEWS FROM PEOPLE WHO ARE NOT MY MOM

If you're new to my ~~work~~ play, you might like to have a quick read of what other books of mine have done to help transform the lives of readers just like you.

I hope Meditate transforms and transcends as much as "Every Single Day" did.

I especially like how "P.C." writes below "There's a **spark** within me that has been relit."

I get my inspiration and content from you and I hope to keep up that connection.

∼

"Somehow, I found myself devouring this today. It's rare that I allow myself this indulgence as the list of what I need to be doing in my head is endless.

Deliciousness to my soul, is the description that comes to mind as I reflect on my experience of consuming this book. I have no idea how to write a review and put into words **how deeply this resonated within me.**

There's a spark within me that has been relit. I know **ESD is the kindling I need to get the fire crackling and roaring** ... there are flames here that need to breathe and light the world.

Thank you Bradley Charbonneau for accepting the challenge of ESD, so that today, you could influence my ESD."

— 5 STARS FROM P.C. VIA AMAZON

∼

"I love how you handle **deep subjects in such a light-hearted way.**"

— Kay Bolden

∼

"**Before reading this book I was ashamed of myself.**

For years I had called myself an artist but I knew the truth. I was only masquerading as one. ... But could I continue to call myself an artist when I stoped making artwork? The answers is no.

I am not entirely sure what happened to me from the time I was in college until now, eight years later. There was **a shift that took place** in my mind during that time.

I **developed a fear** of making artwork. I would always make excuses as to why I just couldn't create. I was too tired, the dog needed a bath, I needed to do dishes. What was the point of painting anyway **because no one would want to buy or look at my work** etc.

I have spent many years working dead end jobs just to pay bills. I **never even allowed myself a chance** at having a career because I would give up at the slightest failure or rejection.

The few times I did really try, I won awards at competitions.

I now have a two-year-old son. I have used him as an **excuse** to not make art for the past two years. I **feel guilty** that I put so much blame on my son. Taking care of him was just a convenient excuse that is easily believed by most people.

After reading this book, there is no going back. I have no choice.

I make artwork everyday and I am happy. ... I know there is no going back.

I was miserable with guilt and now I am not.

I was afraid to create and now I happy to learn once more.

When I started to draw again I was really rusty but I got through it. **I find time** even though I take care of my son all day and I babysit my nephew for eight and a half hours a day.

I wrote this review in the hope that I could inspire someone else to change their life.

Take the Every Single Day challenge. Read this book it just might change your life."

— Paige

"The author shows us how to get past "analysis paralysis" to actually start projects and see them through until completion.

A theme of this book is to **dream about doing something until the dream itself is internalized along with the willingness to progress toward goal completion in iterative steps taken each day.** Readers will learn the importance of getting past inertia in order to begin complex tasks and progress toward a completion date with certainty.

Everyone who moves toward a meritorious goal must first start, stumble, reassess and move ahead with a refined approach toward reaching the goals set forth at the outset. **Very few, if any, tasks are completed with zero failure points or stumbles.** A strong point of the book is that the author sets up readers for roadblocks which must be overcome as part of the learning process. The book could be labelled alternatively as "what it takes to succeed"!"

— Dr. Joseph S. Maresca, Amazon "Hall of Fame" Reviewer

"Maybe you've let your dreams rust.

Author Bradley Charbonneau has published several children's books and travel books, but in this 'self-help' genre he **unveils his own secrets for making life meaningful and successful.**

... the author opens the gates to his pathway for fulfillment and success. '**I transformed myself when I made the decision to change my behavior.**' He places bold statements throughout to make sure he has our attention, phrases such as '**Dreaming the dream was a whole lot easier than living the dream.**'

This fine book encourages us to take a very deep breath, start afresh, and make or lives what they CAN be. A very fine book."

— Grady Harp, Amazon "Hall of Fame" Top 100 Reviewer

∽

"This author has provided an excellent "how to" book, to **move past procrastination**, and **getting past fear**—teaching the reader how things made habitual can result in transformational success. This book could be **a really important read for the new, young person looking to "start" his life journey**, or switch directions after a rocky start. His writing is humorous, friendly, and engaging. I have bought two copies - one for both of my adult children."

— Robert Enzenauer

∽

" ... for anyone with **dreams hidden in the attic, cellar or heart.**"

— Amazon Reviewer

∽

"**He lights a path that you can choose to walk down.**"

— Ray Simon, accomplished speaker, and a no-longer-secret trumpet player

∽

"A **very earnest sharing** by someone who has found his destiny and a way to achieve it."

— Bandaluse

"Half an hour's meditation each day is essential, except when you are busy. Then a full hour is needed."

— Saint Francis de Sales

DEDICATION

For mom

INTRODUCTION

MEDITATE.REPOSSIBLE.COM

"I'm going Beyond the Book."

— Bradley Charbonneau

What you have in your hands is a book. Or maybe you're listening to the audiobook. Awesome possum.

Books are great (writes the writer...) but I have evolved.

Back in 2012, I dreamt of becoming an author. A few long years later (yes, some years are long, some are short, these were long) and kaboom! I'm a writer. This book is my 25th book.

I record my own audiobooks. I love both listening to and narrating audiobooks. Yay for audio! I'm a book narrator.

Since I conquered the author dream, I have broadened my dreams, even dug up past dreams, to become a teacher and a public speaker.

Boom! Doing that now, too.

So I've evolved *Beyond the Book*.

Some people prefer reading. Others would rather listen on audio. Yet others want to watch a video. Some would get the most out of a live workshop or conference.

The Repossible Series is all of that: books, audiobooks, courses, workshops, videos, podcasts, and in-person conferences and retreats.

Believe me, as a writer, I used to think that I could reach the most people in the best way through books. But everyone is different. Personally, I like audio and in-person conferences.

In fact, I smell a numbered list coming…

If I had to prioritize how I like learning and "consuming" knowledge, here's how I would rank it:

1. Small teams, project based (Team)
2. In-person, interactive workshops or retreats (Live)
3. In-person conferences (In Person)
4. Live, interactive online courses (Zoom, with breakout rooms)
5. Audio (Audiobooks, Podcasts)
6. Video (Online Learning, Courses)
7. Books (Ebooks, Paperback)
8. Blog posts (Web Browser)
9. Online PDFs (Computer Viewer/Reader)
10. Printed PDFs (Paper)

The book you're holding is the first step in a whirlwind of future media of learning, collaboration, and cooperation.

We'll have podcast interviews, video presentations, downloadable guided meditations, and more.

It all begins when you sign up at meditate.repossible.com.

- **Possible:** books
- **Impossible:** me presenting in your living room
- **Repossible:** a week retreat in Bali

P.S. It's going to be a continuous flow of new content, events (both online and in-person) and we'll keep adding to it long after you have finished this book.

PROLOGUE

"I'm not super natural. I'm super and I'm natural."

— Bradley Charbonneau

Blah.

That's how I feel right now.

I'm jet lagged, I'm tired, groggy even. I have low energy. My ideas feel flat, my thoughts jumbled.

Even my "Big Ideas" feel ... small.

I think, yes, right now, as I write the prologue to this book, "Who am I to write this book?"

I don't like feeling like this. I don't usually feel like this. For me, this is not my normal state.

But it's how I feel right now.

It's how I used to feel most of the time.

I thought it was normal. Well, it was normal because it's how I felt most of the time. Something that happens "most of the time" is what we learn to accept as normal.

Yet, this is how I used to feel on a regular basis.

With the exception of this jet lag, I rarely feel this low energy, my thoughts are usually clear, even crystal clear. I can quickly distinguish between silly ideas and stratospheric samplings of genius ideas.

At this moment, the only thing I can distinguish is whether I should have water and tea. Even that decision is a hard one (I have both next to me now).

I'm going to go out on a limb here but this is how I think **most people feel**.

About time for a numbered list?

Do you feel:

1. Blah
2. Regular
3. Boring
4. Bored
5. Disinterested
6. Tired
7. Human
8. Mortal

I really shouldn't do this but skip ahead, yep, skip the entire book and go read the Epilogue. If this prologue is the "before" picture then the epilogue is the "after" picture. That's what we're shooting for.

I have to stop this prologue because not only do I not enjoy feeling normal, regular, bored, frustrated, low energy, and mortal, I don't even like writing about it.

Welcome to my world.

Welcome to Repossible.

Welcome to Meditate.

PREFACE
HOW TO USE THIS BOOK

Meditation can transport you to unknown places at unpredictable times based on how much you surrender to your own imagination and desires.

This book is organized in much the same way.

Take a chapter and let it sink in.

Close the book for a day and read another chapter the next day.

You don't need to read it all in one sitting (although it's very short) or even read the chapters in order.

Each chapter is usually its own little story, a little environment of its own world and character to transport you into another time and place.

Many chapters have accompanying Bonus Content which you can find at meditate.repossible.com.

Read a chapter, listen to some audio, watch a video.

Meditation is not a sprint. It's a marathon.

A slow, wonderful, zany trip through the time from when you begin all the way to, hopefully, the rest of your life.

I've been meditating daily since 2015.

This book is a collection from early on when I was getting started to some of the more "out there" experiences from me and other meditators (see the section from guests).

Take a deep breath. Exhale.

Welcome to *Meditate*.

PART I

THIS WILL ONLY TAKE 17 MINUTES

WE ALL HAVE THE MINUTES. IT JUST DEPENDS ON HOW YOU USE THEM.

1

HERE'S HOW TO MEDITATE
JUST KIDDING

"It is always possible to create something original."

— George Gershwin

Sure, I can tell you what I do, but meditation is different for everyone. We'll all (hopefully!) have different experiences. Which is why I'm hesitant here to even pretend to guide you in a meditation practice.

For kicks, here's what I do:

1. After waking up, find a lockable (door) room where I won't be disturbed—the only room in my house is the bathroom!
2. Sit in a chair (I use a terrible, plastic IKEA folding chair that's even broken). I highly recommend NOT meditating in bed.
3. Connect headphones (ideally noise cancelling).
4. Find guided meditation (I use a wide variety from a small group of people I'm happy to share later).
5. Press play.

6. Pull down my eyeshades.
7. Surrender.
8. Don't expect.
9. Be patient.
10. Ask.
11. Play.

There you have it.

If you're just getting started, I'll keep updating links and guided meditations over in the bonus content at meditate.repossible.com but you could try an app on your phone or even just search YouTube for something that resonates with you.

Play. Don't expect. Just give it a go.

- **Possible:** think about the best way to get started
- **Impossible:** start with the best way
- **Repossible:** just try it

2

GUIDED MEDITATION AUDIO: CLARITY
LET THE DULL SAND SETTLE AND FOCUS ON THE SHINY FLAKES OF GOLD

"There are little gems all around us that can hold glimmers of inspiration."

— RICHELLE MEAD

I created an 11-minute meditation for you that walks you through letting go of the overwhelming minutiae of the every day and brings in the glittery flakes of gold that are the gems of our imagination, intelligence, and, once in a while, our powerful higher self.

You have free access to the audio file at meditate-clarity.repossible.com.

- **Possible:** Color in your coloring book with a gold glitter pen
- **Impossible:** Find a lake this morning
- **Repossible:** Join me for 11-minutes of glittery goodness

3
IT'S OK TO HAVE FUN ALONG THE WAY
NO, WAIT. IT'S MANDATORY.

"We believed in our idea - a family park where parents and children could have fun- together."

— Walt Disney

I'm not really in the market for a course or a book or training in:

1. Brushing teeth
2. Eating ice cream
3. Making burritos
4. Walking with my dog
5. Reading

I know how to do those things and I do them well—or at least well enough and I also don't need to become an expert in them.

What are the popular courses out there? I'm going to have a quick glance at popular courses at Udemy. Here's what I found (random top 5 bestsellers according to the home page):

1. Speed Reading
2. Reiki
3. Life Coaching Certificate Course
4. Investing in Stocks
5. Radiate Confidence

With the exception of maybe #5 (confidence), the others aren't things we do "naturally" and, at least not for me, things I do with tons of joy or pleasure.

Well, "life coaching" sounds "fun" to me but that's the teacher in me. I've never really understood the term "Life Coaching."

Whereas here we are in a book called "**Meditate**" and a chapter called "**It's OK to Have Fun Along the Way**" with a subtitle of "**No, wait. It's mandatory.**"

Things we don't like to do become harder to turn into habits. In a way, I feel like I'm "selling" meditation on you in this book. I suppose I am but I'm also trying to let you know that, at least for now, and after a certain amount of time, it has become fun, it does bring me joy and happiness and success and I wouldn't miss it for anything.

It's Obligatory to Have Fun Along the Way

I shop around quite a bit with the guided meditations I listen to. I have my favorites but I like to try out new ones.

I came across some guy the other day on YouTube that was so serious, his voice was so deep, it was as if he was fiddling with the audio filters on his microphone and found one called "God" and then turned up the volume AND the base.

Have you ever noticed that lots of these guru types are often funny? When you get a couple of them together it's almost like a stand-up comedy routine. They're light, they're having a good time, they're clearly enjoying themselves.

There's an hour of audio with Dr. Wayne Dyer and Dr. Deepak Chopra (I think it's called "How to get what you really, really, really want") where they are making fun of each other, cracking jokes, and telling silly stories.

> *"But wait! They're talking about serious stuff! Success, goals, planning, life!"*

Yep, they're joking around.

My meditations have become more and more fun. My dad will drop in and say something completely silly. I occasionally laugh out loud during my meditations.

If you're a light-hearted person (or would like to be!), this chapter is offering you permission to take your meditation lightly, to smile during it, to laugh out loud even, to make it a good time, to celebrate it.

Maybe I can create licenses, like a driver's license, and I can get your photo and your name on there and should anyone ever accuse you of "having too much fun during your meditation" and want to give you a citation, you can show them your license and they'll nod and apologize.

The more you enjoy it, the more it will enjoy you.

- **Possible:** pretend it's supposed to be a serious session
- **Impossible:** take it as earnestly as your tax filing
- **Repossible:** have fun along the way

OK, I could completely see myself making silly licenses like that. If you want one, mention this chapter and send me your name and photo and I'll create something for you.

Maybe I'll start a collection of people's licenses at meditate.repossible.com.

Yes, I might regret this offer...

4

GO IT ALONE. DO IT TOGETHER.
SOLITARILY TOGETHER

"Nowhere can man find a quieter or more untroubled retreat than in his own soul."

— Marcus Aurelius

Meditation is normally a solitary practice. It's usually recommended to do something like:

- Sit alone quietly, with an eye mask, maybe with music or a guided meditation for _ minutes per day.

Yep, I'd go along with that thinking.

However, most breakthroughs I hear about seem to happen in group settings. For example:

- Go on a weekend (or week-long) meditation retreat alone.

Did your parents ever send you off to camp alone? You hoped to bring friends but they suggested you would meet more people if you went alone.

A group setting, especially if you're alone, is a great place to:

1. Meet new people
2. Gather their support
3. Support others
4. Let go of past "personalities"
5. Step into your new self

So while meditation is truly a solitary practice on a regular basis, keep in mind that can be a group event (even an adventure!) where you learn more, get inspired by others, and people won't look at you funny if you tell them you sit on a chair in your bathroom every morning with an eye mask on and listen to a guided meditation for 23 minutes.

Just saying.

- **Possible:** meditate with friends
- **Impossible:** old you + new you
- **Repossible:** go alone, leave together

5

MAKE YOUR OWN NEWS
THE LATEST FROM INSIDE YOUR IMAGINATION

"Some scores from around the league: 5-1, 3-4, 7-2 and 9-6."

— SNL Weekend Update or Steve Martin

Without mentioning a single news item, I'll just say it's June, 2020 as I type this.

Enough said, right?

During the month of June, I was together with my mom and sister as we sat by my mom during the last days of her life.

While I do think it's important to know what's going on in the world (both locally and globally), there are times in life when it's OK to tune it out. Not even just OK, but highly recommended.

> *If I took it just a smidgen further, I would say it should be mandatory: every living human should shut off from all outside news for a month.*

There, I italicized it and centered it, that usually makes things more important, official, and somehow more convincing.

While the citizens of the world dealt with very-real news, my sister and I thought about what music my mom liked and came to the conclusion, after, oh, a lifetime or so that we've been her kids, that our dad was the one who really chose the music and we truly had no idea what kind of music my mom liked or even if she liked certain music more than others.

We looked through photos from past family trips. We made fun of our dad's white running shoes. We made big life decisions at the spur of the moment: should we order Thai or Indian for dinner?

Did you catch that?

While the rest of the planet burned, died, and complained (and I'm really trying here not to "lighten" that hardship—but I am avoiding it both here in this chapter as well as during June), we sat with my mom on her bed and looked through photos, laughed at silly stuff, and devoured Thai yellow curry.

Live! From the inside of your mind!

I can just hear some readers now. In fact, I can hear one perspective of my own opinion. We're saying:

> "Hey Bradley. Hold on a minute. The external world is real. It's where we all live. Are you saying we should just ignore it, hide from it, and pretend we live only in our minds—and hearts?"
>
> — Possibly You

Yes.

That's exactly what I'm saying.

Here's why.

Yes, I keep quoting you without permission but I'm quietly hoping this is something along the lines of what you're thinking you're going to say after you experienced meditation and/or this "other world" that lives in parallel yet somehow separate from the "real world."

"Gee, thank you, Bradley. You gave me permission to escape from the regular, usual, everyday, occasionally negative, often stressed, world that most of us inhabit. You allowed me to discover a place where the "news" is on another level, coming from a different source, and it's all coming from within my heart."

— Hopefully You

Meditation is not 24/7

While that life without the (bad) news of the world might sound appealing, please understand that I in no way mean we all need to move to that mountaintop in Nepal and hide out for the rest of our lives.

Not in the slightest.

I want us to thrive in this world we live in. We can "rise above" the level where most exist. We can float even if just a smidgen higher than the gruff and rumble of the jungle of the everyday by each morning (and/or evening) elevating ourselves to a plane just out of earshot of the "mere mortals" who survive at ground level.

There you have it.

That's the news cycle I want us to be on.

17 minutes per morning of Our Own News to lift our chins up so we can not just survive the day but thrive through it and go to sleep wanting more.

The channel to tune into is your own true frequency.

We just have to adjust the dial and tune in daily.

- **Possible:** ostrich news (hide your head in the sand)
- **Impossible:** all news, all the time
- **Repossible:** make your own news

6

GUIDED MEDITATION AUDIO: CREATIVITY

YOU MIGHT THINK YOU'RE NOT A CREATIVE PERSON. BUT YOU ARE.

"Just when you're about to give up, give in, and give it all back, it arrives."

— Mr. Brad Lee

I don't believe people who say they're not creative.
Sure, I believe that they think they're not.
But they are.
You are.
So there you have it.
Now that you know that, it'll be easier to let this sink in.
You have free access to the audio file at meditate-creativity.repossible.com.

- **Possible:** say you're not a creative person
- **Impossible:** bury your creativity forever
- **Repossible:** creativity doesn't ever leave us

PART II

WHY BOTHER?

SERIOUSLY, CAN'T WE JUST WATCH AN UPLIFTING SHOW ON NETFLIX?

7

THE BEST TIME TO PLANT A TREE WAS 20 YEARS AGO

YEAH, SO THAT'S NOT GOING TO HAPPEN

"I wish I had started meditating sooner."

— Me

I honest and truly don't regret too many things in my life. In fact, I strive to lead a life without (too many) regrets. But if I had to choose one, it would be:

"I wish I had started meditating sooner."

Please note, it wasn't:

1. I wish I earned a million dollars sooner.
2. I wish I moved to Europe sooner.
3. I wish I wrote (more) books sooner.
4. I wish I opened up the first In-N-Out franchise in Europe sooner.*
5. I wish I _____ sooner.

Nope. Sure, some of those would have been nice but regret (and grief and guilt) are emotions I don't need on a regular basis.

Meditation has led to most of the success, happiness, joy, love, appreciation, gratitude, fortune, fame, frolicking freaking fun, and just plain better things in my life.

Yep, I wish I had started meditating sooner.

I started meditating when my dad was diagnosed with cancer and I went on a mission (no, a MISSION) to help him. I went off the deep end and then I went deeper and then I told the lifeguard at the pool, "Hey, I'm going deeper."

I have done 10-day silent meditation Vipassana retreats, 5-day wake-up-at-4-am workshops, and have an at-least-17-minutes-a-day practice since 2015.

You know that cliché "It changed my life." Well, it changed my life.

I write this book mostly just to introduce you to meditation in whatever form you like best.

But if I have a secret sauce, if I were to whisper one word to a seeking soul, the most powerful weapon in my arsenal, it would be meditation.

I don't live on a mountaintop in Nepal. I don't wear purple robes and have dream catcher feather thingies in my windows.

But I make deer appear. I have conversations with my dad. I know what to do in my life, how to do it, when, and why.

I have clarity, peace, joy, love, and I'm working on one of my upcoming books called "Play" because, and I'm sorry if this just doesn't yet do it for you, but life is a game and I'm playing.

With meditation and with life being a game, here's the big takeaway:

"I can't lose."

— BTC

If there's a rulebook, I didn't read it. If there's an instruction manual, I lost it.

There's just one thing you have to do: meditate.

- **Possible:** regret
- **Impossible:** turn back time
- **Repossible:** dare to begin

*This is still absolutely (Re)possible in the future. Just saying.

8

A CASCADE THROUGHOUT THE DAY
WHICH SIDE OF THE BED WILL YOU CHOOSE?

"When you drop any new idea in the pond of the world, you get a ripple effect. You have to be aware that you will be creating a cascade of change."

— Joel A. Barker

You know those days when you just "get out of the wrong side of the bed" and things often go downhill from there? What if there were a way to get up on the "right side of the bed" on a regular basis?

For our human minds, it's often easier to recall the bad stuff, the terrible memories, and even if it was 1 out of 10 times, we remember the one time.

I can clearly remember waking up:

1. With a hangover
2. Wishing the day would hurry up and be over with because "I just know" it's not going to be a good day
3. With a weight on my shoulders
4. With dread

Any of these ring a bell?

The trouble (and the opportunity) with the morning and right when we wake up is that it very often sets the trajectory for the rest of the day.

What if we could begin on a high point and have that goodness trickle down, cascade like a waterfall throughout our day?

Most of us have some sort of morning rituals but many of us do them unconsciously and they are basically the same thing we did the day before. We all do them:

1. Pee (hey, I'm not above the boring necessities of daily reality)
2. Have a (big) glass of water *(hidden pro tip...)*
3. Brush teeth
4. Coffee
5. Breakfast

Something like that?

Maybe some exercise in there somewhere? Read the paper? Check your phone. Oh, maybe I should have put that one first.

No, let's not put "check your phone" first.

Our mornings are more powerful than we realize.

What if there were a pill you could take that would launch the rest of your day into an orbit of energy, joy, positive thoughts, new ideas, and smiles?

Pop a couple of those pills every morning!

Who's going to write that prescription for that medication?

Oops, typo.

I wrote: medication.

I meant to write: meditation.

Crazy how it's just one letter difference, isn't it?

What if your daily morning meditation included meditation?

What if what cascaded throughout your day was not just caffeine, groggy hangovers, and remnants of toothpaste and what you might have done yesterday but a brisk waltz through a morning meadow of mellow mental merriment?

Each of us has 24 hours every single day. Every single one of us will wake up to a choice, a daily simple choice, as to how we're going to begin.

That beginning will reverberate throughout the next 24 hours.

1. Pee.
2. Drink water.
3. Meditate.

When you come up with an alternative 3-step plan for the morning with more potential power for the rest of your day, please share it with us at meditate-morning.repossible.com.

- **Possible:** start your day the same as you did yesterday
- **Impossible:** start perfectly
- **Repossible:** start with good (which can lead to great)

9

THANK YOU, THANK YOU, THANK YOU
IF YOU'RE GOING TO HAVE AN ATTITUDE, YOU MIGHT AS WELL MAKE IT AN ATTITUDE OF GRATITUDE.

"It's not happiness that brings us gratitude. It's gratitude that brings us happiness."

— Anonymous

I used to think things like "Gratitude Journals" were in the same ballpark as feathery dream catchers, unicorns, and pixie dust.

I also had the sorting order wrong. I used to think it was something like:

1. Wish
2. Receive
3. Thank (gratitude)

Now I think it's something like the inverse of that:

1. Thank
2. Wish
3. Receive

Do you know how when you're dreaming sometimes it can be or seem so real that you honest and truly don't know whether it's a dream or if you're awake?

It's a bit like that with gratitude.

You (your mind/self/conscious) doesn't always know if you've done a thing already or haven't yet done it. Yes, of course, you know if you just walked from the front door to the driveway but let's get a little deeper here.

Here's the simplest example I can think of to make the point. Let's say you want to be happy. If you are grateful for ALREADY being happy then your mind is "tricked" into thinking you're already happy because you're thankful or grateful for it.

I know, it doesn't make sense and I wouldn't dare write such things if I hadn't experienced it all myself.

At the beginning of the day, I will often give thanks for something that maybe hasn't happened yet. Maybe it's as simple as a sore throat. Maybe it's as big as a new project or book idea.

I'm thanking, I'm being grateful before it happens so my body can "relax" and "rest assured" that it already happened because I'm thanking for it.

This is one of things where you're not going to believe me—and you're going to think I'm even more of a nutcase—until you do it yourself.

Try it, play with it, work it.

- **Possible:** wish
- **Impossible:** receive
- **Repossible:** thank

10

THE CULT OF YOU
MEMBERSHIP IS EXCLUSIVE, TAILORED, AND FREE

"One person's religion is another person's cult."

— Philip Seymour Hoffman

When people come across something new or weird or even possibly new and weird to them, they want to classify it, categorize it, put it in a box.

When that something involves potential weekend retreats, "mystical" experiences, and other unusual-yet-intriguing adventures, they might be thinking to themselves:

"Yeah, that's probably a cult."

I can't disagree. I don't even really know what a "cult" is. Let's check the dictionary just for fun:

"an instance of great **veneration** of a person, ideal, or thing, especially as manifested by a body of admirers"
 "the object of such **devotion**"

"a group or sect bound together by veneration of the same thing, person, ideal, etc."

— DICTIONARY.COM

OK, so I'm a bit of a language guy but I wasn't sure about "veneration" so let's look that up, too:

"a feeling of awe, respect, etc.; **reverence**"

— DICTIONARY.COM

OK, just one more for reverence:

"a feeling or attitude of **deep respect tinged with awe**; veneration"

— DICTIONARY.COM

Read that one again: *deep respect tinged with awe.*
Seriously, how cool is that?
Remember way back at the beginning of this chapter where we started?

The Cult of You

Remember who else is invited? No one.
What are the requirements to get in? You just need to be you.
Let's add a new requirement to get in:
deep respect tinged with awe
For you. You need to have that respect for yourself. Oh, and tinge it with a splash of awe.
Still with me?
Yes, cults are freaky. Especially the ones that say they're not cults but really are—or are they? Who really cares? If you're part of it, you don't mind what people call it.

But I'm not here promoting some cult in this book. Well, other than The Cult of You.

This is possibly the heart of the entire Repossible Series: **The Cult of You.**

Here's my goal for you (which is the same goal I have for me): self-reliance.

I suppose as an author I'm supposed to do stuff that says, "Buy my books! Join my courses!" but at the end of the day, what I truly want for all of us is self-reliance.

I don't want you to need to rely on me. I don't want to need to rely on you.

I want you to "need" to rely on no one but yourself.

Our own selves have the answers. Through, yes, meditation, we can find much of the trust, guidance, trusted guidance, and, yep, the tinge of awe and a whole bunch of respect.

I get in trouble with my editors (and readers…) for saying this way too often but if you don't pay attention to anything else in this book or the entire Repossible Universe, let this settle in:

> *our goal is to develop a deep respect tinged with awe for ourselves*

Then we are independent. Then we are powerful. Then where do we go for answers? Ourselves! Who has the guidance? Yep, that would be you.

Sure, then we can work together (or rather, play together) and make it all even better but until you have The Cult of You set up and you're a card-carrying member, we can't really move forward all too far.

I love personal development books and courses and podcasts. I read and listen way more than I write. It's fun, it's inspiring. I hope I'm inspiring to you.

But at the end of the day, I'm just on the sidelines cheering you on. You're the one in the race.

Sure, ideally someone is there at the finish line to give you a big hug but when you're sucking air, when your legs feel like hot Jell-O, when you're ready to throw in the towel, who can you turn to? Yourself.

The stronger we make that self, the more we can get help from others to reach new heights, get there faster, and then soar towards new destinations we might not have ever imagined.

There's only one cult you must join. You can even tell people, out loud, right now, as you read this book. Maybe you're on a train or in your living room. You can say:

"Uh oh, this guy Bradley is saying I should join a cult."

— You

But then when the stranger on the train or your partner who's only half listening asks:

"Oh, that's nice. What's the name of the cult?"

— Them

You can smile and with a wink and maybe even something of a horror-film laugh, whisper to them:

"The Cult of Me."

— You

It always makes it real when you whisper it.

- **Possible:** The Cult of Them
- **Impossible:** The Cult of All of Us
- **Repossible:** The Cult of Me

This chapter clearly struck a nerve with me. I can't get over this short phrase: *deep respect tinged with awe.*

I think I'm going to make a banner. Maybe something we could print out.

Done. Check this out: meditate-reverence.repossible.com. Do you have any design ideas to share?

PART III
IT'S NOT ME, IT'S YOU
STORIES FROM THE WILD

11

YOU ARE THE SUBJECT OF THIS BOOK, AFTER ALL

SURE, MY STORIES ARE WILD, BUT I WANT YOURS

"We're so complex; we're mysteries to ourselves; we're difficult to each other. And then storytelling reminds us we're all the same."

— BRAD PITT

Sure, I share some of my deepest, darkest, and most dangerous stories in a section of this book. But what's even more powerful are your stories.

What's Your Meditation Story?

In the following chapters people share their own experiences with meditation. My goal is to keep growing this section and adding to it here (in the book) but also in the bonus content (online).

See more videos, audio, stories, and more but also please share your own story. I'd love to hear your meditation adventures.

Mostly along the lines of:

1. What were you like before you started meditating?
2. What changed that got you to start?

3. Why do you keep at it?
4. Where are you heading? What are you goals, hopes, and dreams with meditation?
5. What advice do you have for others who are just getting started or who are looking to take it to the next level?

Watch, listen, and share your own stories at meditate.repossible.com.

- **Possible:** get inspired by other people's stories
- **Impossible:** live other people's stories
- **Repossible:** inspire others through your own stories

P.S. If you ever need a jolt of energy or a pick-me-up, turn off the news and just watch one of these per day: meditate-joe.repossible.com which will take you, oh, I don't know, more than a year. Just watch one for starters.

12

RELAX

INTO YOUR CORE ENERGY

"Choiceless freedom."

— Hermann Baltes

*E*arly last Sunday morning, after a meditation session, Hermann was on fire. On a roll.

The ideas and words were pouring out of him so fast, he could barely keep up.

He wrote down a list of words that spewed out of him like a firehose:

1. Awareness
2. Intuition
3. Passion
4. Patience
5. Liberation
6. Originality
7. Authenticity
8. Freedom
9. Spirit

10. Serving
11. Being (it might have been "Zenf" which is German for mustard so either I can't read his writing or all of this idea generation was making him hungry)
12. Aliveness
13. United
14. Open
15. Aloneness
16. Togetherness
17. Discovering
18. Being committed
19. Suffering
20. Inspiration
21. Heat
22. Creativity
23. Insight
24. Flow
25. Fear
26. Abundance
27. Love
28. Humility

There's a chapter in this book that promotes the concept of just a single idea per day and how it's enough.

Yet there are days when your cup runneth over, where it just flows and you can't stop it, you don't want to stop it, and you can write or remember or share or just sit back and relish in all of its abundant glory.

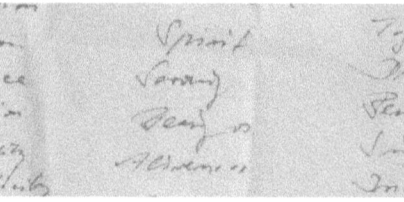

Hermann sits "like a Yogi" on his floor, covers his eyes with an eye mask so it's completely dark, "protects" himself with a blanket and allows only the sounds of the nearby forest to enter his mind.

He makes fun of mindfulness because he's striving for "an empty mind, not a full one!"

He slows down his breath to just above the point where he would, you know, die, and by focusing on his breath, his thoughts dissipate and some of that cherished emptiness comes in.

He doesn't always get 28 "big ideas" but meditation helps him cut through the fat and lift the level of the rest of his day.

Running also works for him but in an opposite way from the slow breathing. Because he's breathing so hard, it's also works in the same way: he's focused on his breath so his thoughts become more clear.

I'm still not really sure if he write "Being" (and then what is that little word after that?) or "Zenf" but I could go for a thick German Bratwurst about now so I'm sticking with Zenf plus I know Hermann will get a kick out of reading about how TERRIBLE his handwriting is and my misguided attempts at humor combined with hunger and a lust for German Bratwurst completely turned this chapter from a deep meditation into frolicking beer-garden level of good times, cheer, and our next book we're doing to write together that he also said happened on that same Sunday morning:

"Relax: Into Your Core Energy"

This is where his term "Choiceless Freedom" came about as he told me we're going to write a book together, he didn't ask me.

I have no choice in the matter yet at the same time, although it seems to contradict itself, I have freedom in the idea that we are going to write a book together.

- **Possible:** one idea per day
- **Impossible:** limit yourself to one idea per day
- **Repossible:** allow more than one idea per day

13

"BETWEEN YOU AND ME, BRADLEY…"
THIS IS GOING TO SOUND CRAZY, BUT…

"Shivers down your spine from your dead neighbor."

— What This Chapter Could Also Be Called

A friend of mine told me about something of what some might call an "out of body experience" but then kept making excuses about how "weird" and "woo woo" it all was.

The same guy who said something like:

"Meditation is a time to reflect, get clarity…"

— The Same Guy

But he also told me about the presence of a person, a deceased person, who "sent a shiver down his spine" and would interject every once in a while as he was telling me this with comments such as:

"I don't know if I really want you to mention my name in your book."

So this neighbor of his, this deceased neighbor, helped my friend with a big decision he (my friend) had to make.

Pretty cool, right? Nice to get advice from people about big decisions.

Oops, except the advice, the message, the help was from a person who is no longer living on this earth.

Do you see the conflict here?

We have a guy, this friend of mine, who:

1. Says meditation is "time to reflect, get clarity," which is great, but then also:
2. Got a message from a dead neighbor.

This is a typical case for most of us who can't quite yet come to terms with any idea that "woo woo" and "messages from dead people" are acceptable and maybe even somewhere near normal so we have to make excuses for them and make sure we know they're not too "crazy" or "weird" or "spiritual" and this was a one-off thing, something out of the blue, and probably won't happen again.

Well, let me tell you: nope, **it won't happen again if you don't want it to.**

So why do we have this hangup with spirituality?

Because it's not:

1. Normal
2. Mainstream
3. Acceptable
4. Who we think we are
5. What we learned in school
6. In the newspapers

You get the idea.

I'm going on and on about my friend because I was in the same position not too long ago.

Now, remember, for the record (see what I did there? I'm "making excuses" for what I'm about to say or how I'm portraying myself), I don't wear flowing robes and tell you I can see your aura and that you should place your left pinky on this crystal and I'll tell you why your uncle Jonathan is really your guardian angel and yes, you should buy his vacation home in Connecticut. No, that's not me.

But I used to be that guy. The one who didn't believe or accept (and certainly not Surrender).

Why am I now this new guy? The one who is OK with friends who get messages from their dear neighbors who have passed away?

Because it's fun.

Because why not?

Because if we only wait for the messages we get through the normal, accepted, and regular channels then we're firing on only some of our cylinders.

Learn to use it, embrace it, secretly, silently, quietly open up to the messages, to the coincidences.

Play with them, see what happens, think about the worst that could happen if maybe it really happened.

It's OK, I won't tell. I won't make your story a chapter in one of my books (well, unless you want me to...).

I'm offering permission to go a little into the deep end of what you believe.

- **Possible:** keep it between you and me
- **Impossible:** keep it to yourself
- **Repossible:** listen to your dead neighbors

14

FROM 1-MINUTE MEDITATIONS IN THE BUS TO SOLVING WORLD PROBLEMS
WITH A LITTLE DETOUR TO TACKLING FORGIVENESS

"One minute was a lot for me. That was the max I could do."

— Sudhanya Mallik

Sudhanya started meditation when she was depressed. *(PRO TIP: so did I. So do many people. Why? We're searching for help. TIP: try to start before you're depressed.)*

On the outside, things seemed fine but somehow, she wasn't happy.

She started meditating in the bus on the way to work. Just one minute (yep, 60 seconds) closing her eyes and trying to see what was going on in her mind.

From just those simple and quick beginnings, she then started:

1. Writing poetry
2. Getting over fear of public speaking (and who she was to dare to speak—and who would listen)
3. Meditating more

Forgiveness

Although this book could be seen as something of an introduction for people who don't have much or any experience with meditation, the beauty of it is there is just so much out there.

After years of experience, Sudhanya found new methods, new directions. One of them was a guided meditation about forgiveness.

After just a single week of this new meditation practice, she said:

"Oh, after just one week, I already feel like it's working."

— SUDHANYA

Let's see if we can sum up a few points to discover here:

1. She started with meditating just 1 **minute per day**
2. This led to **trusting more** in meditation, going further, developing the ability to go 20 minutes
3. She later opened up to new types of meditation and found a guided meditation about forgiveness where she saw **results in a week**

I am fully aware I'm turning this a bit into a numbers theory but I want to show you how easy it can be to get started.

I'll let you listen to her tell you her own experience here: meditate-sudhanya.repossible.com.

- **Possible:** start meditating when you're depressed
- **Impossible:** start when you don't really "need" it
- **Repossible:** start before you really need it

15

TALK TO PEOPLE WHO MEDITATE
LISTEN, (TRY TO) BELIEVE, ACCEPT, GIVE IT A GO YOURSELF

"I believe in soulmates, yes, but I believe you also have to work at love. I happen to believe your soulmate doesn't have to be your partner - your soulmate could be your best friend, your sibling, it doesn't have to be the person you marry."

— CHERYL COLE

In this section, I gathered a collection of different people's experiences with meditation.

This is a tiny sample of people and a minuscule sampling of types of meditations that exist.

In fact, each person's experience is unique.

I believe in the power of story, of storytelling, of experiences shared. "How" someone made you feel is always going to be more powerful than what you learned or when you heard it or sometimes even why it seemed to matter.

> "That person who resonates with you might not be me. But I might share the person's story which does resonate with you."

If you hear a story from someone who aligns with you, one of those people, one of those stories where you say:

"That's me! This person is talking about me! Speaking directly to me as if she knew my own personal story!"

— You When It Hits You

Then you are that much closer to these statements:

1. I believe it's possible
2. I believe it's possible for me

I'll share any audio, video, interviews, snippets or links to podcast episodes where you might just find that one person who whispers in your ear: **this is for you.**

- **Possible:** read the stories in this book
- **Impossible:** hear every story from every person
- **Repossible:** listen for the story that becomes yours

Find them all at meditate.repossible.com.

PART IV

EVERY SINGLE DAY

BRUSH TEETH, ELEVATE YOUR EXISTENCE,
DRINK WATER. NOT NECESSARILY IN THAT
ORDER.

16

WHEN 30 DAYS IS NOT QUITE ENOUGH
IT'S TIME FOR THIS TO SINK IN

"Because 'Every Other Thursday' is too hard to remember."

— BTC from "Every Single Day"

Let's stop tiptoeing around the real issue at hand here. Something like meditation, which is up there with breathing, brushing teeth, and eating as far as "Those Important Habits We Have," isn't just a fad or a temporary phase or even "that thing uncle Bradley was into for a while."

I would say:

"I hate to break it to you but..."

but you see, this is one of those things you're not going to be sorry about. Here's how I really feel:

"Surrender to your higher power."

Wow. Did you catch all that? I just went from (pseudo) apologizing for giving you some "bad news" to allowing you to take the first step towards your greater self.

Please take note that I also didn't say, "Follow Bradley's 87-step plan for awesomeness" or "drink kale shakes every Wednesday" but rather I know—and this I know—that I'm not the answer to your dreams, this book isn't the end-all-be-all of wisdom, and nothing external will get you further than what's internal and I'm not the answer but you are.

You and your higher self.

You and your subconscious.

You and _____ whatever label or name you want to give to that higher self of which you are a part.

Every Single Day

How long do you plan on brushing your teeth daily? Are you going to do it for 6 months and then wind it down to every other day? No.

How about that eating thing? Drinking water? Daily, right?

Breathing? Don't really take a holiday from that transaction, do we?

If you're new to meditation, what if we just gave it a different name? Maybe something like:

1. "Me" time
2. Quality time
3. Connecting with your higher power
4. Rising up to a higher level (of consciousness)
5. Elevating above the "surviving" level up towards "thriving"
6. Tuning into your ridiculously beautiful soul
7. Waking up your superhero self
8. Dialing into 1-800-AWE-SOME
9. Conference calling with the gods
10. A shot of daily energy
11. Downloading from the cloud of all knowledge
12. Firing up the grill of greatness

13. (Please, stop me anytime. This is getting out of hand...)
14. Setting the dial to the frequency of your future personality
15. Finding clarity
16. Surrendering to the energy of your power
17. Stepping into the true love of your heart

Any of those resonate? Got any more you'd like to share? Find this chapter's online cousin at meditate.repossible.com and add your own to the mix.

Pick your favorite from my out-of-hand list above and then choose how often you'd like to do that.

Still stuck on the, "Well, I'm not sure I can find the time..."? If so, pick another from the list and go with that?

Can you see how why I meditate every single day?

What if I miss a day? Is the ESD SWAT team going to bust down my door and take me in for questioning? Not usually, but it's more that I notice my day just didn't go as smoothly, I missed a step, or something just "wasn't quite right."

What if more days were "right" in our lives? What if we listed up just a teensy bit higher than yesterday?

Where you be after a month? A year? A lifetime?

See why I do this everyday? See why I'll never stop?

It's not a race. There is no finish line—other than the daily one. We can't lose.

We might as well have fun on our way from A to B to See.

- **Possible:** every other Thursday for 4 months
- **Impossible:** every single minute
- **Repossible:** every single day

17

FOOD IS A FACTOR
FOR ME, FASTING IS THE FASTBACK TO FREEDOM

"Periodic fasting can help clear up the mind and strengthen the body and the spirit."

— Ezra Taft Benson

My favorite "recipe" for meditation is as follows.

1. Have a normal lunch; get some good protein
2. Drink extra water
3. For "dinner," have an apple or more water
4. Go to sleep several hours earlier than normal, I shoot for 3. So, instead of 11 PM, 8 PM.
5. Wake up 3 hours earlier than normal. Instead of 8 AM, 5 AM.
6. **PRO TIP:** when intermittent fasting, you'll probably find you need less sleep so maybe you can go to bed 2 hours earlier and wake up 3 hours earlier.
7. Meditate longer than normal. If you usually do 20 minutes, do 40 or even 60 minutes.
8. Go about your day.

When we fast, when we have less food to digest during the night while we sleep, our body has more energy left over and we usually wake up earlier, feel more refreshed, and our minds are more clear and ready for something new, unexpected and possibly mystical.

Give the recipe a try and see how you like it.

- **Possible:** feast
- **Impossible:** fake
- **Repossible:** fast

18

ONE IDEA PER DAY
NOT 17, NOT 0. JUST 1.

"People often say that motivation doesn't last. Well, neither does bathing - that's why we recommend it daily."

— Zig Ziglar

*I*t's no-longer-quite-so early on a Sunday morning. My son will be downstairs very soon. I don't have long. It's OK, I don't need a lot of time.

This is one of those simple but not easy things. Let me put it in bullet points to show just how simple it is.

1. I meditate every single morning.
2. I get a new idea almost every time.
3. That idea can usually carry me throughout the day–if not the week, the month, sometimes the entire year.

That's it.

To recap, I get usually at least one new "big" idea per morning. It might be as simple as a new idea towards parenting or maybe a chapter title. It could be as big as an entirely new book idea or even a series.

Maybe even an entirely new service line.

Or my son reaches out for me and says that, yes, he does want my love he just doesn't know how to receive it.

Can you feel me?

Can you sense how one idea is enough? Often, I get more, but one is usually plenty to keep me going, to fill my tank, to generate enough energy, power, motivation, inspiration, and drive to make it happen, get it done, and implement that one thing.

It's that simple.

So I'll stop here and let it sink in.

- **Possible:** one idea (per lifetime)
- **Impossible:** one idea (when you feel like it)
- **Repossible:** one idea (per day)

19

NUMBERS, PROOF, AND ACTION
LET'S DO A LITTLE INVENTORY

"Numbers don't lie. Women lie, men lie, but numbers don't lie."

— MAX HOLLOWAY

There are certainly some "woo woo" chapters in this book. I make deers appear for crying out loud.

But there will be some of you, well, some of us, I should say because I am clearly in the camp of the mathematicians, scientists, and skeptics, who are saying:

"That's great and all, Bradley, but I'm going to need some proof."

— YOU

Here's a quick timeline with numbers:

- 2004 to 2014: 1 book published
- 2015 to 2020: 24 books published

Wanna take a guess as to when I started meditating?

The book you have in your hands is my 25th book. It's 2020 as I write this.

You might ask something like:

"Well, there must have been other factors at play beyond just meditation. What about your Every Single Day writing practice? What about the changes in the publishing industry? What about, you know, other stuff?"

— The Skeptic

Yep, I was skeptical before, too. I also wasn't writing, wasn't happy, and was *dreaming the dream instead of living the dream.*

Then I started meditating and it all changed.

It sounds so simple.

It can't be that simple.

It can be that simple.

It is so simple.

- **Possible:** wait 10 years
- **Impossible:** start 10 years earlier
- **Repossible:** meditate starting now

20

CANDLELIGHT DINNER ON THE EIFFEL TOWER
YEAH, SO THAT'S PROBABLY NOT GOING TO HAPPEN ON A DAILY BASIS. OR WILL IT?

"The sky is the daily bread of the eyes."

— RALPH WALDO EMERSON

We spend a disproportionate amount of time wishing, dreaming, hoping, fantasizing, imagining, and pretending our evening will end with that famed candlelight dinner on the Eiffel Tower.

You know the one: you stare deep into her eyes, you hold her hand, every word you say probably will be made into a movie or a poetry collection (or both). At just the right moment, fireworks explode near you illuminating the sky—and her face—and you know this evening will be the most romantic, adventurous, and deliriously splendorific of your entire life—if not of multiple lifetimes.

Then you wake up.

Yeah, cuz that's probably not going to happen.

At least not offscreen in, you know, real life.

I worry that my 14-year-old compares real life to her Playstation existence. In real life, the explosions just aren't as big, murdering the bad guys doesn't happen every hour, and you can't start over when you feel like it.

But how much do we also, as adults, strive for that postcard perfect scene? The sunset on the white sand beach? The yellow street lamps of a sleepy Greek island? The dinner on the Eiffel Tower?

Sure, they might happen every now and again but if we spend 94% of our time NOT living those fantasies and that same 94% of our time feeling:

- disappointed
- regretful
- cheated
- hopeful

then we are waiting to "live" only the 6% of time that we're actually in some postcard scene (if that much, your numbers may vary).

AKA How To Transform Your Bathroom into Paris

Sure, I'd rather spend the morning waking up in Paris but for the most part, I wake up in my own bed in my own house.

> **PRO TIP:** *wake up half an hour earlier at home than you would in Paris.*

Now if you're following along here, you might think I'm going to get into how to turn your bathroom (or wherever you meditate) into a warmly-lit pied-à-terre in Paris.

Sure, we could do that.

In fact, if Paris is what you're striving for, then by all means, meditate your way to Paris.

In fact, I used to do that. I would use visualization to transport me to living in Europe.

Oops.

It worked.

But now I live in a place I want to live (I don't want to live in Paris, I lived there, that was enough, it's more fun to visit!), so what can I meditate about? What or where can I be transported to in my morning meditation?

I can go wherever I want.

I can transform my bathroom into a place, a time, a state of being, a collection of memories, a vision of the future, and even ask my dad what he thinks about what happened yesterday.

Paris is the tip of the iceberg.

What we can see or visit or understand during meditation goes far beyond a geographical pin on a map.

I used Paris in the example (or Greece or wherever it is you'd love to be) to make it something we can visualize. But the fun part of meditation is when you get past the "normal" stuff (money, travel, etc.) and get into the unknown.

What if you went to the travel agent (as if anyone does that anymore…) and asked them:

"Where will you send me today?

— You asking angelic travel agent

What if you were open to transform your bathroom into something more exotic than Paris? More "out there" than a place on the world map? Deeper inside of you than you've ever been? Further in space and time than you imagined even possible?

Can you tell the train to Paris has left the station?

If you get me started with:

"Where would you like to go today?"

And you mention meditation in the same sentence that's when things get a whole lot more interesting than being asked the same question at the airport.

But first, let's get back to basics.

Where would you like to "go" this morning? Where will your meditation take you?

Close your eyes and go.

- **Possible:** put a lavender bar of soap in your bathroom
- **Impossible:** wake up in Paris (when you went to sleep in your own bed)
- **Repossible:** meditate beyond only a physical place

21

THE PASSION TO _____ HAS TO BE GREATER THAN THE FEAR OF _____
FOR EXAMPLE: INSERT "LIVE" AND "DEATH"

> "He said to me, 'Oh, uh, there won't be any money, but when you die, on your deathbed, you will receive total consciousness.' So I've got that going for me, which is nice."
>
> — Carl Spackler, relating what the Dalai Lama told him (after he caddied for him)(yes, I quote from Caddyshack often and defiantly)

*T*his is going to be a quick chapter but it's also one of the most powerful, basic, and necessary.

It's going to sound simple (and it is) but let's say your fear about, oh, I don't know, **writing a book** is that it will be:

1. Terrible
2. Read by no one
3. Ridiculed by The New York Times AND your neighbor (who says often 'I'm going to write a book someday')
4. A complete failure
5. Laughed at because YOU wrote it and who are you to dare write such a book?

(Can you tell I've experienced just a couple of these first hand? They *never* go away...)

OK, now that I've succeeded in scaring and depressing you, that's the **fear** part.

The trick with meditation (and with most things) is that the **passion to do it** (in this case, to write the book) has to be greater than the **fear to not do it.**

There you have it.

It really is that simple.

This quote, this idea comes from a deeper place:

> *"The passion to live has to be greater than the fear of death."*

But you can apply it to your meditation.

> *PRO TIP: Well, it's not even a PRO TIP, it's a necessary tip but it's so important I'm labeling it PRO. Your meditation passion is easier to change/increase to become bigger than your daily life fear.*

Did you catch that part? That was the important part.

During your meditation, you need to see, gauge, and/or make the passion greater than the fear.

So there you have it. It's a biggie. Take a minute to digest and talk amongst yourselves.

- **Possible:** fear of _____ greater than passion to _____
- **Impossible:** no passion, no fear
- **Repossible:** passion to _____ greater than fear of _____

22

THE RADIO SIGNAL IS ALWAYS TRANSMITTING
THE QUESTION IS WHETHER YOU ARE RECEIVING

"Sometimes I think the surest sign that intelligent life exists elsewhere in the universe is that none of it has tried to contact us."

— BILL WATTERSON

When I was a kid, for the life of me I couldn't figure out how the voices came out of the radio.

It just kept going, too. Where were the voices coming from? How did they get in there?

"So many voices! All those stations, some with multiple people talking!"

— YOUNG BRADLEY, NOT QUITE UNDERSTANDING RADIOS AND WAVELENGTHS AND RADIO WAVES

When I moved to Germany, I thought back to when I was a kid because here the same box now spoke German, too!

Another note from a baffled kid: how does a dog hear a dog whistle? How come we can't? How do we know it's working?

What still freaks me out is that I can turn on a radio and it just picks up the signal.

As if the signal is always around us, consistently on, constantly surrounding us as if it's waiting for us to turn on the radio, adjust the dial and tune in.

Oops.

The signal is **always on**. It's **around us**. All we have to do is **turn on the radio** and **tune the dial into the right station**.

The biggest revelation with meditation and connecting and tuning in was this radio metaphor.

Once I learned or figured out that the signal was always on, forever transmitting, and there for the taking, everything became easier.

It's not that we are the big transmission station. We are the receiver. It doesn't "cost" us any energy to pick up the signal. We just turn on and tune in.

This is a radio.

This is meditation.

- **Possible:** wait for the radio to turn on
- **Impossible:** tune to all stations
- **Repossible:** find your station

PART V

SO THIS HAPPENED

NOTES FROM THE DEEP END

23

OUT OF THE SPIRITUAL CLOSET
YOU'RE NOT GOING TO BELIEVE THIS BUT…

> "You're not going to believe this, but…"
>
> — Often the first line of emails to staff at Encephalon
> (Joe Dispenza)

We're in book number seven of the Repossible series. I think it's OK if I'm going to "go off the deep end" a bit, maybe even "come out of the spiritual closet" and dare share things I wouldn't dared even told Pepper only a few short years ago.

In the next few chapters, I'm going to dare share with you a few experiences from my own meditation practice.

I do this because:

1. It's out of my comfort zone (because you might think I'm crazy/weird)
2. You might quietly and/or secretly resonate with some of the experiences because you've had them yourself
3. You haven't yet had such experiences yet you'd like to and reading about mine might allow you to begin such adventures for yourself

Just because I like to build the drama, remember that I hold an MBA from a prestigious European university, I implemented SAP for a technology consulting firm, and my favorite subject in school was mathematics (especially statistics and reason and logic).

I mention these "professional credentials" for those types (like my dad and the former me) who are going to read the next chapters and want to toss me out with the bathwater as some purple feather, flowing robe nut job who has clearly spent one too many early mornings surrounded by gongs and chanting monks.

Yeah, I've done that, too.

If you're not ready for it, skip the next chapters.

If you think you're not ready, dip your toe in the water.

If you'd like to share your own stories, we'd love to hear them at meditate.repossible.com because what I'd really like to see this section of the book (and the online bonus content) turn into is a collection of people's "Out of the Spiritual Closet" stories of adventure, mysticism, and whatever it is that you see when you close your eyes.

See you on the other side.

- **Possible:** hide from the world
- **Impossible:** hide from yourself
- **Repossible:** come out of the (spiritual) closet

24

OH DEER

OH DEAR, IT'S A DEER.

"The true scientist no longer attempts to disprove the pull of gravity, or the rotation of the earth, or the motion of heavenly bodies, or the sequence of the seasons, or man's need of food and water, or the function of the heart."

— Ezra Taft Benson

I was with my wife and son in the woods. We had just been talking about basketball, of course, and I "slipped away" for less than a minute to see if my mom was around.

I took maybe 15 seconds and asked:

"Alright, mom. I'm here. Where are you?"

— BTC

The path turned slightly to the left and then I saw it. A deer. Seemingly waiting for me to see her.

She didn't rush off right away but waited until she was sure I acknowledged her presence.

There you have how it happened.

Now let's get into why it happened.

There are two theories, neither of which are provable.

Theory #1: Coincidence

Yep, Bradley, you called out to your recently deceased mother and within seconds a deer appeared.

Yet, in logical thinking, action #1 (calling out to my mom) does not cause the reaction #2 (deer appears).

I cannot prove my action caused this reaction.

However, I also cannot disprove it. You cannot prove my action was not the cause for the reaction.

Theory #2: Not Coincidence

Same action and reaction:

1. I ask mom to make an appearance
2. Deer shows up

What if, just if there were the craziest possibility, that me calling out, me asking, seeking, making the request, somehow triggered some force, some "thing," some I-honestly-don't-know-what to make the deer appear?

I can't prove it but I also can't disprove it.

Let's ask then the more important question:

"Which of these two theories is more fun?"

— You Ask

Did you notice the question was not:

1. Which of these two theories makes the most sense?
2. Which of these two theories will be one day proved by science?
3. Which of these two theories would my wife believe?
4. Which of these two theories am I going to admit to at the dinner party?
5. Which of these two theories do I want to believe?
6. Which of these two theories do I honest and truly believe?
7. Which of these two theories matters?

Maybe it's me. Maybe I'm the guy who writes a book called "Play." Maybe this is coming from a guy who likes to talk about the nine lives of cats and remind us that we, the humans who can do things like read books but don't seem to have the whole nine lives thing going on, have just this one life and why should we spend time on something that can't be proven or disproven and we can freely choose a side and we won't have to defend it in court, at dinner, or even in bed but we can secretly "believe" or even "make-believe" that this is the way the universe, the world, our world works, and what harm does it do to think in such a way?

There you have it. That pretty much sums up my Philosophy On Life (and well, Death) since my dad passed away.

Why not believe? Why not enjoy that it *might* be like this? What's the worst that could happen?

Let me tell you: oh, I don't know, someone says, "That's silly."

Then you smile, nod, and move on.

Yet that deer was there. I saw it. I took a photo. That photo is above. Pepper didn't even notice her.

How did she get there? Why did she show up at that moment in the history of time? On that path, in that forest, right in front of me?

You don't have to tell anyone which theory you believe. You don't have to tell your spouse, your neighbor, or your kids.

There's only one person you have to whisper it to. You'll do it with a sly smile that often turns into a little laugh because you can't believe you just told yourself you believe in this stuff.

That one person is, of course, no, it's not me.

It's you.

- **Possible:** oh dear
- **Impossible:** oh deer
- **Repossible:** oh dear, it's a deer

But if you do tell me, I won't tell anyone. It'll be our secret.

25

RUPERT

THIS IS WHAT I DID ON A FRIDAY MORNING

"Make them feel welcome, included, like a part of the family."

— Rupert, from Zimbabwe

I'm not even sure would believe anyone who told this tale and yet here I am telling it.

I'm not even sure I would believe myself except that, you know, it just happened this morning.

So there's that.

If I hadn't turned on the voice recorder right after my meditation, I doubt I would have ever believed it.

Oh, one more thing.

I'm going to go out on a limb and guess that many people think meditation is some "nice" thing you do to, I don't know, be at peace with the world and walk in dandelion fields and drink cloudy tea from half a coconut shell.

For the most part, I do it for the adventure. Like this morning.

But, as you'll hear, I do it for the "business ideas," the actionable steps to take in building, creating a business, getting new clients, paying partners, finding more ways to incentivize collaborators even more so it's a win-win-win situation: win for the new audience, win for the ambassador, and win for Repossible.

Win win win.

Can't be all bad?

It's not even any bad.

In fact, it's all good.

Listen in to my morning where I meet Rupert (meditate-rupert.repossible.com).

Enjoy my "trip" to Zimbabwe.

- **Possible:** oh dear
- **Impossible:** oh deer
- **Repossible:** meet Rupert

26

I'M A DRUG DEALER

IF THIS WERE A DRUG, I'D INJECT IT DAILY

"If you can't find the ideas or don't know which ones are the good ones, or want different and better ones, here's one solution."

— BTC

What you have below is what I wrote on a Sunday morning after a meditation. I share this with you in a way to *prove* to you, to walk the talk, to share with you not only the *crazy* stuff but the *good* stuff, where the *awesome* ideas come from (HINT: it's the same place where the terrible ideas come from!) and let you into my head in order to let yourself out of your own head and to invite you to experience the weirdness, the beauty, and seriously, the fun that meditation can be.

Here goes.

Don't say I didn't warn you.

∼

IT'S SUNDAY MORNING. Everyone is still asleep and I need to write as fast as I can to possibly get 1/2 of the goods I just had delivered to me.

No, not the UPS guy on an early Sunday morning.

The "downloads" from my meditation.

I just spent 1 hour and 15 minutes in deep (and WAY FUN) meditation. I got so much from it that I'm exploding with ideas. Some awesome, some *who knows*, and others I will have forgotten by the time I get to the end of this post. By the way, that's perfectly OK, let those go and keep what sticks.

> "I write this in early 2020 as a potential chapter for my upcoming book, aptly named "Meditate." It's book #7 in the Repossible series and is probably the most powerful. Yep, you need to Ask and you need to Dare to get going. You're going to want to Create and Spark that creativity in others but if you're looking to up your game, to take it to next level and then really take it to a level you've possibly never even heard of, then you're going to want to do this. Just saying. OK, back to trying to scribble down as fast as I can what I just experienced."
>
> — BTC

Long ago, I surrendered to the idea that I bother thinking of who reads this and who I might offend or, better yet, who I might resonate with and change their lives.

With that said, I'm not holding back.

In only the order as it comes off of my fingers...

I'm a Drug Dealer

- TED talk
- Toastmasters competition speech
- FB video ad

I have (at least) 2 things going on in the coming months:

1. Spark
2. Toastmasters

I have a 90-second video of an 8-year-old girl who is opening up the author copies of her first book. It's heart-wrenching, it's inspiring, it's, well, hard to believe that an 8-year-old girl published a book. Here it is:

https://youtu.be/AwJuvzRx_ew

She's 8. She's an author.

Here's my plan.

I have speeches (talks, presentations) to give for Toastmasters in the coming weeks and months. It's contest season so I need to sharpen, dig deep, and blow away the audience. Well, I suppose I don't "need" to do that, but I want to.

The talks are between 5 and 7 minutes. I thought of putting the video above into slow motion, remove my audio of course, and then talk over it as the audience sees her opening the cardboard box.

They, of course, don't know what she's doing.

I open by saying

"I'm Bradley Charbonneau and I'm a Drug Dealer."

-- *Yeah, that would be me.*

That's compelling, right? We're just getting started.

Now I'd need to do some research but my play on words is that I'm dealing in "drugs" or chemicals like these:

1. **Adrenaline:** butterflies in the stomach
2. **Dopamine:** exquisite delight in all the smallest details
3. **Serotonin:** you feel significant or important
4. **Oxytocin:** creates intimacy, trust, and strengthens relationships
5. **Endorphins:** helps to alleviate anxiety

See where I'm going with this? I could even pause the video as I go through and point out when the "timed release" of my wonder drug (that is to say, SPARK) releases and activates the body.

Could also do a 90-second version as FB or even Pinterest ad. Ooh, I like this.

Ooh, so daring, so fun, so good. OK, gotta move on. More to come here.

Every Single Day Playbook

A workbook, no, playbook, to accompany (and help expand) the success of my Every Single Day book.

I quickly saw a few versions.

1. **Paperback:** "30 Days from Work to Play" (ooh, I just thought of that one right now, I LIKE it) is a paper workbook that I'm calling a "playbook" because it's not work. Which is one of the main themes.
2. **Online (drip campaign) course:** 30 days of emails (and/or videos or "lessons" or activities) to accompany or complement the paper. Or paper is good on its own and this is separate for non-paper people.
3. **Free online course:** a 10-day (maybe 5-day) shorter version of the above to introduce people to my work, I mean, my play.
4. **Ebook:** I don't know if this is such a good idea but a digital version of the paperback mostly to lead people to the online course and/or paperback. Could give away this for free or charge for the book and give big discount (or even 100% discount) to online 30-day course.

I Need Help. I Need You. I Need a Team.

A marketing team, an operations crew, collaborators who can help implement this.

I feel like I'm halfway through my meditation and I'm so enthusiastic about the ideas above but I know more and more that I need a team.

This will probably sound odd but hey, it's Sunday morning and I'm in a state of clarity so I'm going to go with it.

If I were already "famous" and a "big name" and had a following of gazillions this point would be moot. I would have people reading this and clamoring to be a part of it.

But I'm not there yet.

The thing is that I want to build this team before I get there. I think this team, these ambassadors, these co-creators, are part of what will propel this upward, onward, and to places I (on my own) can't even envision.

I need you. Join me? Let's **talk**.

Side Note: my wife is now up, my youngest will come in here any minute. This is why I get this done first thing in the morning.

I Can See

I close my eyes to see.

> "**WARNING:** In the interest of clarity, I'm going to go full-speed ahead with what I get out of these meditations. From your perspective, I might be now heading into "Woo Woo Land" and if you need to get up and stretch your legs, feel free to make your exit. But frankly, this is where things get juicy and, I can't believe I'm saying this but this is where things get good."
>
> — Me

During my meditations, one technique is to **ask who needs help**. I let all of my own ideas and thoughts fall to the floor and whoosh away easily.

This morning, my oldest son came to me and wanted to show me something in his heart.

He had to peel back the layers and it took some effort but he got there and said something like:

> "See, I have a heart and it's full of love. It's there and it needs more love. I have so much love to give but I don't know how to give it and

it scares me to give it not knowing if I'll be laughed at or if that love won't come back to me."

— My Son

If you're still reading this, these are the sorts of things I experience in my meditations.

Often, my dad or even lately my grandfather (who I barely knew) will come in and offer help or guidance or often talk to me about whoever is there with me.

If I read into this what does my son need? What is he asking for?

He has a big heart and he "wants to use it" but maybe doesn't know how or he's scared or it's behind so many layers (what are those layers made of?) that he doesn't do it and he hides and remains in the shadows.

This gets a little graphic but hey, it's a meditation, I don't really ask questions about the "how in the hell is this happening?" but go with it and see what happens. I open my entire chest exposing my own heart and my gut. It's all open, wide open, and I let him in there and take what he needs but also see that I'm open and offering anything and everything I have to him.

It's all for him, I have so much, I have so much to give and so much to share.

He nods and thinks he might understand and has something of an attitude of, "OK, I guess I see how that works." which isn't unlike his attitude towards math homework.

But I have offered and sent my love to him and showered him, covered him with my love and let him know he has access to it anytime and all time.

So yeah, there's all that.

Surrender

I give in to something larger, bigger, "more" than the singular me.

Part of meditation is the "download" where it comes to you, you gather or collect the information (like what I've outlined above) but then there's that nit-picky little element of actually getting it done.

Towards the end of the meditation, I will release everything that's arrived towards, yeah, this is where things get a little murky, but to a greater self. Maybe that's a greater/larger version of myself, maybe it's you, maybe it's some celestial being, maybe I'm sending it up to the ceiling and it's stuck.

You know, I'm trying to be funny and light and silly, but I have to say: it doesn't get stuck at the ceiling.

It does go higher. I don't know where it goes exactly but this part of the process is not letting it rest on only my shoulders. I give it up, I give it away, I put it up "for auction" to see who's there and who can help.

It "releases" it for me and allows me to glide, to roll and delight in the ideas and worry and stress less (if at all) about it actually getting done.

As I type this, I realize it might sound like I'm giving up on the work, that I don't care if it gets done. I don't know how to explain it but it's not that. It's truly letting go and "seeing what happens" with it.

I'm going to leave good enough alone here for now.

OK, that's it for today

This was one single morning for an hour.

Can you imagine this every single day? What if you had this clarity, this download of information and advice and tips and strategies and who-knows-what-I've-already-forgotten in the hour I've been writing this down as best I can?

Can you imagine you had access to this?

Every day, you had a window into the world, into your own world of your own power. Without distractions or if they do come, you embrace them and smother them so they either go away or turn into something you needed to deal with.

Oh, had I found meditation when I was 20. Or 10. Or 30.

If I knew of a more powerful drug, I would inject it daily.

If I could buy an apparatus or machine that got me a fraction of what I get out of this, I would order it for next-day delivery.

But I don't have to wait.

I don't have to order it.

I just need to put on my headphones, close my eyes, and let the power come to me.

Have a great Sunday.

I know I will.

- **Possible:** oh dear
- **Impossible:** oh deer
- **Repossible:** oh dear, it's a deer

27

TINY KEYS LODGED IN HIS BACK
A TRIP INTO A MORNING MEDITATION

"The highest of distinctions is service to others."

— KING GEORGE VI

Tiny ones, big ones, all wedged in there.

My son sighed and let his shoulders slump as if to say, "Duh, I can't do that. Here's why."

He lifted his hand, turned it, and pointed behind him but a little bit downwards as if on his back.

I didn't know what he was getting at so I moved to where I could see his back.

Inserted into his back were keys. They looked like old keys from old houses where they're big and simple, but also beautiful and solid.

There were little ones and then big ones. Mostly copper or gold or rusted metal. Maybe they'd been there a while.

We communicated as we often do without words and he got across to me that he couldn't necessarily so easily do what I was saying or suggesting because these keys were lodged in his back and they represented habits or actions from the past that are determining his future.

Mr. Solution here thought:

"Well, let's just take them out."

— Mr. Solution aka Me

But not all of them were bad or wrong or necessarily needed to be removed. They were his past, after all, for better or worse. But they were his habits and thoughts and they were influencing his present and his future.

How did we know which ones to remove and which ones to let be?

I waved my hands around his back slowly, as if scanning or feeling for something, anything. As I did it, a few of the smaller keys wriggled themselves loose and came to my hand as if they were magnetized.

"Hey," he called out but quietly and curious. "What are you doing?"

Before I answered, I waved my hand once more and again some of the keys dislodged and came to my hand. I put my hand down low and shook my wrist as you do when there's not a towel in the bathroom after you wash your hands. The keys dropped and disappeared.

"I'm just getting rid of some of these old keys you don't need anymore," I said.

He was cautious but deep down, he trusts me. He knows I'm in this for his best interests.

But for me, it was a visual version of how our past influences our present and our future.

What's holding us back? What's guiding us, consulting us, leading us and based on what information or experience? Can we change our habits? Can we remove some of those keys–even the bigger ones–and go about things in a different way in the present and future?

Based on how a few of the keys came out pretty easily, it seems so.

Which keys are "turning on" your decisions? Which ones do you need to get rid of?

"Yep, this is a daring foray into my meditation and just one of the experiences I have on a daily basis because I open up, I allow the visuals and stories and messages to come through. I think I'm filing this under the series *Meditate*."

— Early Morning Bradley

- **Possible:** meditate
- **Impossible:** help only yourself
- **Repossible:** meditate to (eventually) help others (once you've got yourself in a good place)

PART VI

NOW WHAT?

ALL THIS READING IS GREAT AND ALL BUT ...

28

IT'S TIME TO MAKE TIME
YOU'LL GET THE TIME BACK EXPONENTIALLY

"Lost time is never found again."

— Benjamin Franklin

I write a lot of books. I have loads ideas. People ask me about stuff and I tell them stuff.

"Stuff." I know, I'm so scientific.

But you see, I **am** scientific.

I know your answers are not within me. In fact, I know exactly where they are—and so do you.

They're within you.

How do you get them?

If you know how already, awesome possum. If not, I'd suggest meditating.

That's it.

That's my big final chapter here.

I kinda go a little off the rails (no, me?) in the Epilogue. If you're not quite feeling that motivation, go read the Epilogue.

But things are about done for me.

It's now time for you.

- **Possible:** start when you're "ready"
- **Impossible:** start yesterday
- **Repossible:** start today

EPILOGUE

"This can't be real."

— BTC

There's a chapter in this book that is a perfect example of what I hope you will get out of it: *we can live on a higher level*.

That one chapter was inspired by a guy who started out with, "Bradley, between you and me..." and continued to tell me about his "woo woo" experience of getting a message from an old friend of his his.

An old friend who had passed away.

In other words, are you holding onto your hats here? He got a message from a dead person.

I add this "unbelievable" story of spirituality gone wild here in the epilogue because if at the simplest level of a meditation practice, we:

1. might get some clarity in our lives,

2. maybe reduce some stress,
3. and possibly go from surviving to thriving

yet at the height of a meditation practice we're getting decision-making help from those who are no longer living then I have done my job here.

We don't need to hide from it, we don't need to be embarrassed about it, yet we also don't need to shout it from the rooftops that we've achieved it, we've ascended to it, that we're there and live there, thrive there on a daily basis.

I certainly don't want to cram it down your throat that You Must Meditate! but rather I hope only to broaden your perspective with what *might happen* should you give it a try.

In the prologue of this book, I talked about how I was jet lagged, felt tired, how my thoughts and ideas were flat and I just didn't have much energy.

That prologue is the exception. I rarely feel like that anymore.

It's been at least 4 paragraphs since we've had a numbered list so here goes a collection of terms that I have collected around meditation:

1. Clarity
2. Focus
3. Smiles
4. Joy
5. Delight
6. Fantasy (into reality)
7. Dreams (come true)
8. Inspiration
9. Motivation
10. "One (big) idea per day"
11. Thriving
12. "If I don't do it, who will?"
13. Why not me?
14. Let's get going

15. Power
16. Trust
17. Faith
18. Certainty
19. Delight (Oops, I already mentioned that one. I'm leaving it as it deserves at least two spots.)

I'm going to copy and paste the numbered list from the prologue here for kicks:

1. Blah
2. Regular
3. Boring
4. Bored
5. Disinterested
6. Tired
7. Human
8. Mortal

Which list are you feeling closer to?
I'm not saying that meditation is the answer to everything but ...
OK, fine.
I admit it.
I'm saying meditation is the answer to everything.
I wish you could see me as I type this. I'm laughing. It's one of those "knowing" laughs where I have tears in my eyes because it gives me such energy and joy and certainty to write about this, to know this, to share this with you.

My delightful designer, Anne Mitchelson, commented about my books that she really liked the quotes I collect and drop into the beginning of each chapter but that they also "took the reader away" from my voice, my style, and my flow.

At the beginning of this epilogue, yep, I did it: I quoted myself. I said, "This can't be real."

Take the example of the guy who got the message from his

deceased friend. The message that gave him some clarity in a big decision he

ACKNOWLEDGMENTS

Had my **dad** not had his cancer diagnosis, I might have still been flailing about without purpose, wondering when that lightning would strike to guide me towards my life's mission, and quietly regretful that I wasn't yet the person I had always dreamed of being. But when he got sick, I went looking for answers and found meditation.

I want to acknowledge a **doctor** who scared me to death (well, clearly not literally) with her predictions and forecasts and possibilities and numbers and chances and when I said I learned of someone who had reversed a diagnosis through meditation (and other means) and then she said:

"Well, that's just one person."

and I thought, but didn't say and only said it aloud later when I was less scared, less in a mode of surviving and had transformed into a mode of thriving would I have loved to have said something as witty and deep and powerful as:

"How many people do you see standing before you?"

But I didn't say that yet I thought it however later I realized I only needed to help one single person and that one person was me. So how hard could that be?

So I want to thank that doctor because she helped me help that one person (me) and that one person can now help others.

I also want to thank **Pepper** (yes, my dog) because if he didn't need to pee and poop so often, I would certainly not be as often as I am in the forest and in the forest is where I become magical, powerful, where lightning strikes and where the thunder rumbles. So thanks, Pepper.

If you're still reading all the way down here, past my vague references to doctors and gods (WOW, I just I'm-not-dyslexic-but-I-typed-god-instead-of-dog) and, well, I'll leave the **gods** in there and add dogs, too, but what I was getting as was acknowledging **you**.

See how now both **gods** and **you** are bolded in the paragraph? That wasn't intentional but now it is.

This is a perfect example of how creating (in this example, me writing this Acknowledgements chapter) leads to the unknown, the unexpected, and you come across stuff, seemingly accidentally yet possibly not coincidentally, and here I am putting gods and you in the same paragraph because where I was starting out with with you, to acknowledge you for reading down this far as most people won't yet the ones who do are the ones for whom meditation can work because that's just it: it's simple but not always easy. You have to "work" at it until it becomes "play."

You have to put in the 17-minute mornings to get to the crazy, mind-blowing, week-long fantastical adventures that meditation can bring.

But you have to do the regular stuff, the boring daily stuff that might seem endless and worthless and just a pure waste of time but since you're down here, buried in the acknowledgements, I think you're going to find the gems, you'll uncover the sparkling wonders, and you'll find a way to turn it all into play.

I acknowledge **you**.

RELATIONSHIP

Building a relationship with readers is one of the best things about writing.

I occasionally send an email with details about **new books, sneak peeks** into Works In Progress, early bird **deals**, as well as exclusive, **Readers Only insights** into the writing and publishing process.

For Spark, it all lights up at spark.repossible.com.

ABOUT THE AUTHOR

I think I gave up writing this in the third person a few books ago.

I wrote this fantabulous "About the Author" chapter but then it was such an inspired introduction to meditation that I moved it over to the chapter called "The best time to plant a tree was 20 years ago."

Because that's my main goal with this book: to have you dip your toe in a meditation practice and I wanted to get all of that inspiration early on in this book.

As I write this new version of the About the Author chapter, I'm thinking mostly about my mom who passed away last month.

I'm going to copy and paste a few sentences from a boy (now a man!) my mom helped over the years. He was a high school student in Kenya and my mom found him through some NGO but eventually went directly to him. She helped him financially with his studies but they also emailed on a regular basis.

Here's what he wrote when he learned of my mom's passing:

"I don't know what to say Leah...am sorry for the loss..Dede coming to my life was the best thing that ever happen to me..so bad that I'll never meet her in person and thank her for changing my life..Everything i have ...Everything I'll ever have in my life it's because of her...The last 11 years have been the best for...i knew i had someone i could count on....not only for financial help but one i could talk to...She was the best..I will miss her..I wish she was there to write me one last time."

— C.O. (FROM KENYA)

My screen just got blurry as the tears stream down my face.

They never even met in person and yet he writes how my mom changed his life.

If at any point in my life, someone is changed or helped or improved by something I did or said or wrote then my life is complete.

Then if someone else says it, my life is a bonus.

Then someone else? It's all just frosting.

Wayne Dyer asked:

"How may I serve?"

My mom, whether daring to stand up in front of gnarly 7th graders, raising her own children, or supporting a single boy in Kenya halfway around the world, served.

She left some enormous shoes to fill but I see it as my goal in life to serve, to help those whom I can somehow help, to teach anything useful I have learned, to share my energy, my passion, my love to those who seek it.

I hope this book opens up the world of meditation to you and that you reach out to me and let me know if my words, my thoughts, those of my mom, or of this boy from Kenya, helped you in any way, even the slightest way, a teensy-tiny smidgen of an improvement and then my life, your life, our lives are that much more full of love.

A woman at a conference I attended recently shared that all she really needed earlier in her life was someone to stand up and say *I love you* to her.

She said we could do this easily and say it to people, even people we don't really know and what harm could it do, anyway?

She then said, "OK, watch this. Here's how easy it is. I'll go first. Are you ready? I love you."

So. I'll start.

Are you ready?

I love you.

This is my twenty-fifth book.

It is far, far, far from my last.

Find, ask, dare, create, and play at:
bradleycharbonneau.com

facebook.com/bradley.charbonneau.author
twitter.com/brathocha
instagram.com/brathocha
amazon.com/author/bradleycharbonneau
goodreads.com/bradleycharbonneau
bookbub.com/profile/bradley-charbonneau
linkedin.com/in/likoma
pinterest.com/likoma

ALSO BY BRADLEY CHARBONNEAU

Most of my books are also available as audiobooks (which I giddily narrate). Search for my name at your favorite audiobook distributor, slip on your headphones, and let me take you away.

Repossible

Repossible

Every Single Day (+ Playbook)

Ask

Dare

Create

Decide

Meditate

Spark

Surrender

Play

Celebrate

Evaluate

Elevate

Frequency

Every Single Day

Every Single Day Playbook

Every Single Day Kids

Every Single Day Teens (I want to write this one because I want to read this one...)

Every Single Day Parents

Charlie Holiday

Now Is Your Chance (1)

Second Chance (2)

Chance of a Lifetime (3)

For Creatives

Audio for Authors

Meditation for Creatives (2020)

Shorts

Secret Bus to Paradise

Where I (Already) Am

Pass the Sour Cream

A Trip to Hel

Drive-By Dropping

Li & Lu

The Secret of Kite Hill (1)

The Secret of Markree Castle (2)

The Key to Markree Castle (3)

The Gift of Markree Castle (4)

Driehoek (5)

Really Old ...

urban travel guide SAN FRANCISCO

THE END

Thank you for reading "Meditate." Books don't often have "The End" anymore, so I thought I'd make sure we're really done here.

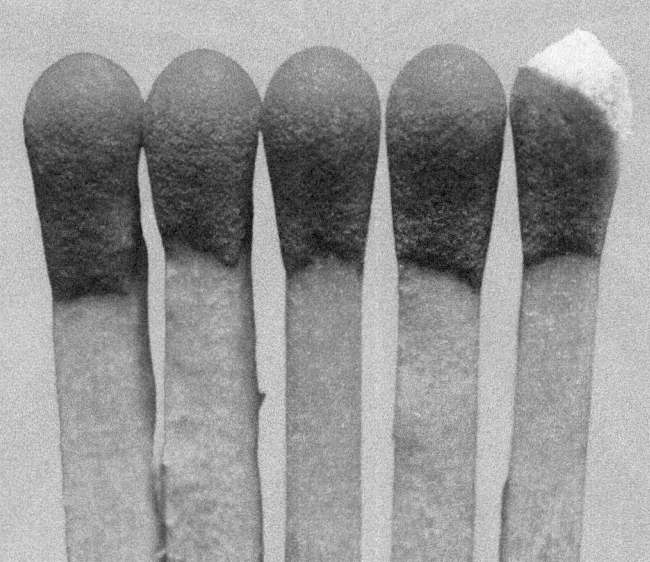

REPOSSIBLE BOOK 8

SPARK

IGNITE INITIATIVE. WE'RE BETTER TOGETHER.

BRADLEY CHARBONNEAU

PRAISE FOR EVERY SINGLE DAY
A QUICK SELECTION OF BOOK REVIEWS FROM PEOPLE WHO ARE NOT MY MOM

If you're new to my ~~work~~ play, you might like to have a quick read of what other books of mine have done to help transform the lives of readers just like you.

I hope Spark transforms and transcends as much as "Every Single Day" did.

I especially like how "P.C." writes below "There's a **spark** within me that has been relit."

I get my inspiration and content from you and I hope to keep up that connection.

"Somehow, I found myself devouring this today. It's rare that I allow myself this indulgence as the list of what I need to be doing in my head is endless.

Deliciousness to my soul, is the description that comes to mind as I reflect on my experience of consuming this book. I have no idea how to write a review and put into words **how deeply this resonated within me.**

There's a spark within me that has been relit. I know **ESD is the kindling I need to get the fire crackling and roaring** ... there are flames here that need to breathe and light the world.

Thank you Bradley Charbonneau for accepting the challenge of ESD, so that today, you could influence my ESD."

— 5 STARS FROM P.C. VIA AMAZON

"I love how you handle **deep subjects in such a light-hearted way.**"

— Kay Bolden

~

"**Before reading this book I was ashamed of myself.**

For years I had called myself an artist but I knew the truth. I was only masquerading as one. ... But could I continue to call myself an artist when I stoped making artwork? The answers is no.

I am not entirely sure what happened to me from the time I was in college until now, eight years later. There was **a shift that took place** in my mind during that time.

I **developed a fear** of making artwork. I would always make excuses as to why I just couldn't create. I was too tired, the dog needed a bath, I needed to do dishes. What was the point of painting anyway **because no one would want to buy or look at my work** etc.

I have spent many years working dead end jobs just to pay bills. I **never even allowed myself a chance** at having a career because I would give up at the slightest failure or rejection.

The few times I did really try, I won awards at competitions.

I now have a two-year-old son. I have used him as an **excuse** to not make art for the past two years. **I feel guilty** that I put so much blame on my son. Taking care of him was just a convenient excuse that is easily believed by most people.

After reading this book, there is no going back. I have no choice.

I make artwork everyday and I am happy. ... I know there is no going back.

I was miserable with guilt and now I am not.

I was afraid to create and now I happy to learn once more.

When I started to draw again I was really rusty but I got through it. **I find time** even though I take care of my son all day and I babysit my nephew for eight and a half hours a day.

I wrote this review in the hope that I could inspire someone else to change their life.

Take the Every Single Day challenge. Read this book it just might change your life."

— Paige

"The author shows us how to get past "**analysis paralysis**" to actually start projects and see them through until completion.

A theme of this book is to **dream about doing something until the dream itself is internalized along with the willingness to progress toward goal completion in iterative steps taken each day.** Readers will learn the importance of getting past inertia in order to begin complex tasks and progress toward a completion date with certainty.

Everyone who moves toward a meritorious goal must first start, stumble, reassess and move ahead with a refined approach toward reaching the goals set forth at the outset. **Very few, if any, tasks are completed with zero failure points or stumbles.** A strong point of the book is that the author sets up readers for roadblocks which must be overcome as part of the learning process. The book could be labelled alternatively as "what it takes to succeed"!"

— Dr. Joseph S. Maresca, Amazon "Hall of Fame" Reviewer

"Maybe you've let your dreams rust.

Author Bradley Charbonneau has published several children's books and travel books, but in this 'self-help' genre he **unveils his own secrets for making life meaningful and successful.**

... the author opens the gates to his pathway for fulfillment and success. '**I transformed myself when I made the decision to change my behavior.**' He places bold statements throughout to make sure he has our attention, phrases such as '**Dreaming the dream was a whole lot easier than living the dream.**'

This fine book encourages us to take a very deep breath, start afresh, and make or lives what they CAN be. A very fine book."

— Grady Harp, Amazon "Hall of Fame" Top 100 Reviewer

"This author has provided an excellent "how to" book, to **move past procrastination**, and **getting past fear**—teaching the reader how things made habitual can result in transformational success. This book could be **a really important read for the new, young person looking to "start" his life journey**, or switch directions after a rocky start. His writing is humorous, friendly, and engaging. I have bought two copies - one for both of my adult children."

— Robert Enzenauer

" ... for anyone with **dreams hidden in the attic, cellar or heart.**"

— Amazon Reviewer

"He lights a path that you can choose to walk down."

— Ray Simon, accomplished speaker, and a no-longer-secret trumpet player

"A **very earnest sharing** by someone who has found his destiny and a way to achieve it."

— Bandaluse

"With patience and persistence, even the smallest act of discipleship or the tiniest ember of belief can become a blazing bonfire of a consecrated life. In fact, that's how most bonfires begin - as a simple spark."

— Dieter F. Uchtdorf

DEDICATION
FOR LI & LU

Well, but also for Pepper.
Without Pepper, we never would have had one of those orange and blue bouncy balls and "The Secret of Kite Hill" might never have been discovered.

A Note about Li & Lu

My wife Saskia and I have two sons: Li & Lu. Those aren't their real names. I'm choosing to use their stage names in order to keep the flow of the story going.

But it's also to protect them from the paparazzi. With the probable future breakout success of the Li & Lu series, it's only fair to protect them as a father and potential tour manager should.

They are both available for interviews anytime. However, Wednesday evenings are basketball practice for Lu and Li needs to catch up on his math homework if he wants to achieve the levels of secret mathematical wisdom displayed in book five of the series, "Driehoek."

If you'd like to contact them directly, you can probably find them on Instagram although they rarely (OK fine, never) post about their literary

achievements and it's usually more along the lines of photos with fries and expensive sneakers.
This book is for them.

PROLOGUE

In March of 2014, I wrote "The Secret of Kite Hill" together with my two sons (then 8 and 10 years old).
　It was both "just a fun little thing we did" and a "monumental shift in who I was" at the time.
　This is precisely my point, my philosophy, and my drive.
　As cheesy as the cliché is, that little book changed my life.
　A silly little 38-page story about walking home from school with the dog.
　But it wasn't the book itself that did it.
　It was the process.
　It was reading chapters aloud as they lay nestled in their beds—even on a school night.
　It was Lu asking, after I had finished reading a chapter, "Then what happened?" only to have me respond that I didn't know because it was *his* story and what happened would have to be created in his own imagination.
　It was getting them to sit down and record the audiobook version (no chips here).
　It was bribing them with tortilla chips for non-audio-recording sessions.

It was whining and pleading, "No, dad. Not the book project again!"

It was Li building a book trailer on our brand-new iPad.

It was determination.

It was creating something from nothing.

It was afterwards when my too-cool-for-school older son said to his buddies (and didn't know I was within earshot), "Yeah, I have a book on Amazon."

It was the "Side Effects" of the action taken.

It was the "Hidden and Unknown Benefits" of co-creating.

It was starting, muddling through, persevering, and getting something finished. We got it *done*.

Together with two young boys.

This is my story.

This is their story.

This is the stories of others who have traveled a similar path.

My hope with this book is that it becomes your story.

Welcome to Spark.

FOREWORD
BY GAVIN REESE

"The world always seems brighter when you've just made something that wasn't there before."

— Neil Gaiman

This is an important book, maybe the most important you'll read this year. I don't believe I could possibly overstate the significance of what Bradley's shared with the rest of us, but I'll leave it to you to decide. For me, this is most important concept in nearly a decade.

Spark is about relationships, connections, and quality time spent with the most important people in your life. Whether you're considering putting this to work with your kids, grandkids, nieces, or nephews, we're all searching for ways to capture the moments of their growth, encapsulate them, and ensure we keep a piece of time that never gets to grow up. The process Bradley explains in Spark does just that. The most beautiful aspect of this is that you aren't required to be an author, writer, or wordsmith to make this work for you and yours. It helps, but it isn't necessary. The end product is not the mark of success here. It is only the journey getting there that matters at all.

I struggled to find ways to engage with the kids in our family for years. How do I get them to put down the tablet, turn off the TV, engage in an actual dialogue, and spend quality time with us before they grow up and these opportunities are lost forever? They all quickly grew tired of me asking what they'd learned each day in school, and I had grown equally tired of the one-word responses to my investigation of their lives. How it is that all the kids I know never learn anything in school each day?

I can't say that all those obstacles forever changed after I met Bradley and put his co-author process to work, but I can tell you that our family has a new hobby. Together. Everyone's engaged, willing, and eager, even if they're a little too cool to openly show it all the time.

I grew up in a divorced family, and I've always wanted to have that romanticized experience with my dad in which we rebuilt a car together. Beyond the refurbished hot rod, we'd have this block of time, a few months spent together over a few years, that can't be lost no matter what happens to the car. Spark can help you and your treasured littles have that same experience. Hours, days even, spread over weeks and months creating something together that everyone's excited about and happy to be a part of. You won't have a 1957 Chevy Bel Air two-door post at the end, but you will have a book. A document that forever records what your little's life was like at that moment in time. Repeat this every year or so, and you'll have a catalogue history of their growth and development. More importantly, you'll have the memories of doing this together. Those moments can never be taken away, regardless of what life and the world have in store for all of you.

See? I told you this book was important. It has been for me and it can be for you.

-- Gavin Reese, author of multiple thriller series and co-author of Space Dogs with his niece, Maddi Lager.

PART I
WHY

"Because your imagination can change the world."

— Neil Gaiman

1
INTRODUCTION: EMBERS

> "At times our own light goes out and is rekindled by a spark from another person. Each of us has cause to think with deep gratitude of those who have lighted the flame within us."
>
> — Albert Schweitzer

Although this book is supposedly about kids and for kids, I'm going to let you in on a little secret early on. Yes, I realize we're in the introduction of part one of the book, but hear me out. I'll be brief.

We, dear parents, dear adults, are the ones who probably need the spark.

Yep, this entire book started out with the intention of rekindling that spark within our children. But you know what? They are like, if you'll excuse my tireless visuals of fire and kindling and embers, that perfectly constructed bonfire with the pine needles and thin strips of bark gathered so carefully. It's all ready to go. There's just enough air and fuel and all it needs is a little spark.

Meanwhile, we adults are more like that smoldering pile of wet charcoal the night after the bonfire. Then it rained.

As I've worked on this book, interviewed moms and uncles, bakers and musicians, authors and artists, I've learned that although the kids might need that one little spark to get the fire started, we are the ones who are going to bask in the warm glow of the adventure, this experiment, this time in our lives.

Meanwhile, once that fire has caught, they're looking for marshmallows and a stick to roast them on.

They have the energy, the creativity, and the bottomless imaginations. We're here to provide that initial spark to get this campfire started.

We're after the lasting, glowing, and warm embers that will endure far beyond this one scene in the long play of our lives--and the many acts to come for our kids.

Embers. Warm. Glowing. Alive.

That's why we're doing this.

2

THE QUARTER-INCH DRILL BIT, SPARKS, AND EXPECTATIONS
NO, REALLY, WHAT ARE WE AFTER HERE?

"No one buys a quarter-inch drill bit because they need a quarter-inch drill bit. What they need is a quarter-inch hole."

— Ted Levitt

In an interview with Tim Ferris on his podcast, Seth Godin explains Ted Levitt's quarter-inch drill bit theory.

"What you need is a place to put the books that are cluttering your bedroom. But you don't even really need that. What you need is the way you will feel when your spouse thanks you for cleaning things up. What you really need are safety and security and a feeling that you did something that was important."

— Seth Godin

What are we after here, anyway?

As Seth Godin says over and over, "No one wants to buy a quarter-inch drill bit." People don't lay awake at night dreaming about it.

They don't talk to their friends about it. They don't really care about the drill bit.

What do they want?

In his example: praise from his wife. A feeling of pride. Safety and security.

In a book about writing a book with your kids, I really shouldn't say this, but... it's not about the book. It's about with the kids.

Then there's that last bit from Seth Godin, "a feeling that you did something that was important."

There you have it. The big secret of this book: a feeling that you did something that was important.

When it comes down to it, that's what I'm after.

If you'd like to know what I'm after, it's even easier. It's the same thing. For me, it's a feeling that something I did was important if I can help you feel like something you did was important.

That's it.

The rest is details and process and deciding and willpower and scheduling and deciding to make this happen. Deciding that you're going to be one of those people who do things like this.

What are things like this?

Something we feel is important.

Flashback

On the actual Kite Hill itself, San Francisco, California

> *"Who's going to buy a book about our stupid story on Kite Hill anyway?" asked Lu. He had a point.*
> *What I couldn't quite eloquently (or effectively) explain to my then 8-year-old son was that the book wasn't what I was after. What I was after was the experience of working on the book together with him and his brother.*

3

MESSAGE IN A BOTTLE

IF DREAMS ARE TRAPPED INSIDE AND AREN'T LET OUT, ARE THEY STILL REAL?

"It's the possibility of having a dream come true that makes life interesting."

— Paulo Coelho

When dreams come true I imagine fireworks and tears of joy and some kid with a huge grin on her face.

This, of course, is after the dream was created, given permission to exist, and realized.

But what about those dreams that are still bottled up inside of a child (or worse: an adult) that were never given permission to come out and play?

Frankly, I wonder what's worse: to have started a dream and never quite achieved it? Or to have never let the genie out of the bottle to see what happens?

They both sound pretty awful to me.

Which is why I want to set them free. Make sure we pull them out of our kids even when we might think they're stuck.

You know that nasty hair in the shower drain? You think you just have a little bit of it and you pull it up but then you get this big, nasty glob of hair?

The dreams of your child might be like that. Hiding out in the drain of the shower needing just the tiniest of extra efforts and patience to set it free.

Is it time to check the shower drain?

Is it time to check what dreams might be stuck in your child?

Is it time to check what dreams might be stuck in you?

4

LET'S CREATE A FAMILY TRADITION
PICK A BOOK, ANY BOOK. READ PAGE ONE.

"It's true, Christmas can feel like a lot of work, particularly for mothers. But when you look back on all the Christmases in your life, you'll find you've created family traditions and lasting memories. Those memories, good and bad, are really what help to keep a family together over the long haul."

— Caroline Kennedy

That was it. Nothing earth shattering. Just trying to make every night a little special, just add a little spice, just a little something to remind us that we're alive, that each day, that each night of our lives is a little different if we choose to make it so.

No, it didn't turn into an annual tradition. In fact, we never did it again. But this book isn't so much about me and my family and what worked and what didn't. It's about sprinkling ideas into you and your family and seeing what sticks, what works, what flops, and just giving it a shot.

It's mostly about giving it a shot.

Flashback

Haunted house of books. Santa Barbara, California

We're staying in a friend of a friend's house that must have thousands of books. They're everywhere. It's an old house with more character than Meryl Streep. We're only spending one night, but I think I could spend a year. It's going to be hard to leave tomorrow.

We got home late and it's just the boys and I and I didn't want to go right to sleep.

How do you begin traditions? Something that you do with your family every year. Who thinks it up? Who keeps it going? Just start. See what happens.

Before I lost their attention, there were just so many books. What could we do with them? There was a front room with cozy chairs and something of a loveseat. The whole place was a throwback at least 50 years. All as if it hadn't been touched in 50 years.

"OK, let's all read page one of whatever book you pick up. Just read it to yourself. Then we can tell each other what it was about. OK?"

I was surprised, but they went for it.

Li got "To Kill a Mockingbird." Lu got something about London streets and I got "For Whom the Bell Tolls."

We all read in silence for a few minutes and then explained what we had read.

5

RINA

A MEAN CORNBREAD AND THE ONE RECIPE COOKBOOK

"I think in terms of chapters. Every time I finish a movie, it's a chapter. When one of my kids graduates from school, that's a chapter."

— STEVEN SPIELBERG

Rina is something of a perfectionist. She's an excellent photographer, but will wait for just the right light, or until the child turns slightly and then she's got it.

Everything she does has style to it. It's beautiful, inspiring, and complete.

While we were brainstorming about "Spark" experiments for her and her children, she brought up the idea of a cookbook.

"My boys can make a mean cornbread," Rina said with pride.

We talked more and I could see her dreaming up the photography for the book, the perfect font to use for each recipe heading. She'd probably dig up old family recipes and add a splash of the nature of her children to combine the old with the new.

"How many recipes do you need for a cookbook?" she asked as we walked in the forest.

In a rare flash of brilliance and mathematical wizardry, I calculated how long it was going to take her to do the photo shoots, lay out the pages properly, get her kids to look just right while stirring the cornbread dough, multiplied all of that by the number of family recipes to be added in and then calculated time for editing and retouching of photos and I had her answer.

"One," I said as someone with far more experience in cookbook publishing than I have and a generous helping of one of my larger goals: Get It Done.

Her jaw fell, her eyes widened, and her shoulders dropped as the pressure was removed from the scene.

Instead of loading her up with a lengthy project, hardbound cover production, and a heaping spoonful of responsibility, I gave her permission.

Permission to play.

To make this fun. To Get This Done. Done is Won.

One chapter. One recipe. One photo for all I care. Here, Rina, we'll even give you some title options:

1. Two Boys and their Dough
2. Cornbread Like You've Never Tasted
3. The One Recipe Cookbook: Cornbread
4. Kids' Kornbread Kookbook
5. Cornbread for Kids

We're still in the Why section of this book. I'll probably hammer you over the head with this, but I want us to FINISH a project.

I don't want Rina to make the perfect cookbook with 43 recipes from 8 generations on 256 glossy pages that will show up on my doorstep in the year 2037.

We're building a time capsule and you don't keep adding to those. You do it, bury it, and move on.

The one-recipe cookbook will be in stores as soon as...uh, Rina?

PART II

WHO

"I have no special talent. I am only passionately curious."

— Albert Einstein

INTRODUCTION: CAMPERS

"Fires can't be made with dead embers, nor can enthusiasm be stirred by spiritless men. Enthusiasm in our daily work lightens effort and turns even labor into pleasant tasks."

— JAMES BALDWIN

et's do a little roll call:

1. **You?** Here! (reading these words)
2. **Me?** Check. (writing these words)
3. **Them?** Present! (probably not right here, right now, but they're around somewhere)

Oh good, we're all here.

1. **You:** parent, aunt, grandfather, adult of some kind.
2. **Me:** parent, uncle, occasional adult, author of this book and five other books I wrote together with my kids.
3. **Them:** kids. They don't even need to be yours. If you don't

have a daughter or son, a niece or nephew or Samantha down the street all work just fine.

I already don't like the "us" versus "them" I seemingly have going on in my numbered list above. My goal is to transform all of us into a communal "we."

This section is called "Who" and I just wanted to make sure we're checked in at the same campground. You might think that I'll stop at some point with the whole "spark" and "ember" and "campfire" mentions. But I won't.

7

THE WIDOW AND THE ORPHAN
EVEN JUST THE TITLE OF THIS CHAPTER MAKES ME WANT TO WRITE A STORY.

"The way to connect to people is to relate to who they are and do something that stretches you outside of your comfort zone."

— STACY BROWN-PHILPOT

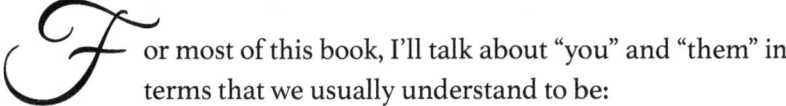or most of this book, I'll talk about "you" and "them" in terms that we usually understand to be:

1. Parent
2. Child

But it could very easily be:

1. Uncle and niece,
2. Single guy and neighbor kid,
3. or how about widow and orphan?

I have a specific person in mind with this concept. She's 94 years old and is sharp as a tack. She has stories to tell until the cows come home (and long after they've gone to sleep). She has more energy than most people a quarter of her age and I've only ever heard the following request in the presence of her:

"Could you slow down grandma? We can't keep up."

She's a machine.

Here's a wild thought for Spark: what if we could connect widows and orphans? Widowers and the girl down the street who doesn't really connect with her parents?

I'm not talking about adoption. I'm talking about a 1-month, start-to-finish, short book they'd create together.

What if Spark brought together two strangers who then collaborated on something? Who knows, maybe the chemistry didn't quite gel and it fizzled out after a week.

But what if something happened?

They met a few times and started to talk. The little girl wanted to tell a story about her doll and her dog and how they talk to each other but nobody ever wanted to listen.

What if the old man in the senior living community listened intently to the girl and whispered to her, "I can hear them talking now, Nina, but I can't quite understand what they're saying. Could you translate for me?"

Can you see the story sparkling to life in front of the girl's eyes? Her imagination would explode and she would have a captive audience who truly wanted to hear her story and what the doll was saying to the dog.

In 30 days, they'd have a finished book. Things got a little out of hand and the old man eventually called in the nurse to transcribe everything the girl was saying in the story as his hands got tired from all that writing. The three of them sat around the lunch table and "The Adventures of Fifi and Fido" came to life.

Grandpa and the nurse thought things were all good and done until the next time the little girl came by and said, "I have another story. Could you help me again?"

I see Sparks flying, embers warming, and moving in closer to the campfire to get going on book number two in the "Fifi & Fido" series.

Do you know anyone in a senior living community who might like to connect? How about a child who could use an ear to listen?

Maybe we could make this work. Let me know if you have any ideas at spark.repossible.com.

8

GAVIN

DON'T HAVE SON OR DAUGHTER OF YOUR OWN? NOT A PROBLEM.

"The hidden child wants to be able to participate and to co-create in art, rather than being simply an admiring viewer."

— Christian Morgenstern

What I love about Gavin's story is that he doesn't have a son or daughter--but he has a niece. I mention this because it opened up (like Grand Canyon-size open) my dreams about where the Spark project could go and immediately addresses comments I've had from adults without kids who say, "But I don't have kids." Also, see the chapter titled, "The Widow and The Orphan."

Here's how Gavin began:

My then-seven-year-old niece, Maddi, loves books, and she'd shown some interest in my burgeoning writing career and occasionally asked questions about it.

"She'd show some interest" is the key phrase here. Pounce on any interest kids show (or try to hide!) and run with it.

Here's more directly from Gavin:

> Maddi freely offered her opinions and wants, so I guided the dialogue and our objectives to ensure the story had a simple plot, some tension, and positive resolution. We also needed a catchy, unusual title, which she provided: Space Dogs. Within a few minutes, we created a project in which she was intellectually interested and emotionally invested.

I'm going to highlight again: "intellectually interested and emotionally invested."

I'd venture to say that we only need one of those two:

1. Intellectually interested
2. Emotionally invested

If you can get both, you're pretty much set. But if I had to pick one, I think "emotionally invested" might get you further. Let's add a body part to Gavin's list:

1. Intellectually interested (brain)
2. Emotionally invested (heart)

This entire operation, in my humble opinion, is an adventure of and for the heart. Yep, we'll learn some things and probably become a better writer or negotiator or story teller or illustrator along the way but what I'm after is the heart.

Back to Gavin:

> Dostoevsky, it ain't. It's not supposed to be. It's a very simple and short story, but it fulfilled every objective I had at the outset of this project. Maddi contributed to a dialogue, an intellectual back-and-forth that required compromise and consideration of someone else's wants, thoughts, and opinions.

- Objectives? Check.
- Dialogue? Got it.
- Intellectual back-and-forth? Yep.

But then comes The Good Part. Gavin explains:

For me, this is very closely akin to the 1957 Bel Air two-door post that my dad and I haven't ever rebuilt together. It's an incredibly important, emotional anchor in our relationship. No matter what happens over the rest of our lifetimes, we'll have these moments we got to spend together. Nothing can take that away from us.

Can I do another bullet list?

- Emotional anchor? Check.
- Moments we got to spend together? Yep.
- Nothing can take that away from us. Got it.

I'm thrilled Maddi had some "intellectual back-and-forth." I'm not even sure how often I have "intellectual back-and-forth."

But the tear-in-my-eye-inducing "Nothing can take that away from us." is the experience of it, the co-creating they did, the dare-I-say "project completion" of working on something together, pulling through, and getting it done. Together.

I'm going to give you just a bit more of Gavin and drop in a teaser from their book:

The plot revolved around our extended family's collection of dogs. All but a few are lovable mutts, but a couple real-life scalawags among them had created tension that helped us craft the story. Two of our heroes had trouble getting along with another species; their differences were just too great to be friends. They decided to travel to space to seek out wisdom from other dogs that had found ways to befriend different creatures. They quickly acquired this new knowledge, returned home to Earth, and told everyone what they'd learned. All dogs live happily ever after.

All dogs live happily ever after? I think Maddi is onto something. Stay tuned for the sequel...

9

LIFO: LAST IN, FIRST OUT
YOU CAN'T FINISH IF YOU DON'T START.

"Finish last in your league and they call you idiot. Finish last in medical school and they call you doctor."

— Abe Lemons

Yeah, sorry for the "Last In, First Out" reference. It's from a production line in a factory. You see, I went to business school. Got a master's degree even. I feel like I have to throw around my knowledge sometimes to remind myself why I had to drudge through accounting for two years. I also need to grant myself the key to take off my necktie, to not take life so seriously, to get into the dirt with the kids, to think like they think, to let go of adult complexities, forget the degrees on the wall, and give myself permission to play. That's who we are allowed to be--or become.

Back to LIFO...

Think of a parking lot. Did you ever go to a game where it was so poorly organized that people just parked behind each other and if you got there last, you were going to have to get out first? That's Last In, First Out.

First In, First Out could be that same ballgame parking lot but then they open the (front) gates so those who got there first need to leave first. Another typical First In, First Out is a factory assembly line.

So the product (or in this case, your project) might be Last In, but there's a chance it's First Out. In other words, you might be a little late getting started, but **the fact that you're starting increases your chance of finishing.**

How much?

I'm going to call it a 100% increase. How do I know? It's easy math. If you don't start, your chances of finishing are 0%. If you start, your chances increase from 0 to 1. Although, mathematically, just starting doesn't mean you'll finish. But not starting does equate to not being able to finish.

Where in the world am I going with this chapter? (That's a rhetorical question that I better answer in the next paragraph or I'm in trouble.)

If you're last in, you might truly be first out. Maybe you've procrastinated and hemmed and hawed and now have a better idea of what you're going to do and finally, somehow, from somewhere, maybe even from reading this chapter, you know you're going to do it.

You now have motivation, momentum, and you're more in a hurry than you were before.

You're not late to the party if the party is still going. You arrived. Now your party can start.

∼

Flashback
Antelope Canyon, Motel Parking Lot, Page, Arizona
I have a pang of pain that I started all of this too late. My kids are getting older. I'm getting older. Maybe I missed the window of opportunity. I try not to worry about things I don't have control of. I also try not to regret what I cannot change. I'm reminded to keep going, to keep playing the game.

10

MAGGIE

HANDS UP: WHO HAS A LIFE GOAL TO WRITE A NOVEL BEFORE YOU'RE 50?

"A dream you dream alone is only a dream. A dream you dream together is reality."

— Yoko Ono

We're still in the section called Who. Although many (most?) of us might think this is all for the kids, we adults are not only active participants in the experiment, but we may well be the accidental subject.

Maggie writes for a living. In fact, many professionals write for a living: attorneys write up cases, doctors write reports, and managers write business plans. She's a professor at a university and her writing is nonfiction.

But Maggie wanted to write fiction. She also wanted to do it before she was 50.

- Enter stage left: Josh (son).
- Enter stage right: Matt (husband).

Now I don't know if Maggie's dream was to sit on her porch, sip iced tea, gaze out onto the lake, spend 14 years, and write the Great American Novel.

When you dare to co-create and make the project a team effort, flexibility is key.

Her husband Matt relates how it played out:

> "It dawned on us that Maggie is a prolific writer in her profession (at a university). I'm an engineer at an aerospace company that understands physics."

Now the part where Maggie and Matt's story takes a turn down the creative path is what he says next. Because from the view on the sidelines, I'm pretty sure no one is yet seeing a clear path towards writing a book together.

> "We thought we could teach physics to children along with telling a really fun story. Maggie's got all the writing skills, I've got all the physics."

This is clearly a family after my own mathematics-loving heart. Only a select few would have "teach physics" and "children" and "fun story" in the same sentence. It was obvious we were going to get along.

Then their son Josh comes into the picture.

> "Josh can tell us what references work for a 8-12 year old kids. What's funny, what isn't funny. What references are good, what references are way too old."
>
> "We really have the three people we need to write a successful book."

They took their diverse backgrounds and calculated that they had what they needed.

I feel a little math coming on:

1. A university professor
2. An aerospace engineer
3. An 11-year-old boy

That's doesn't scream, "I know! They should write a book together!" It doesn't add up.

But can you follow me here with where this is going?

It does add up.

It adds up perfectly.

1 + 1 + 1 = 3

Then we get into exponential mathematics--and things get really good.

Maggie is fulfilling her dream of writing fiction before she's 50.

Matt said the book project improved his marriage and he got to write some science fiction to boot.

Josh is thrilled to be their sounding board and "editorial consultant."

1 + 1 + 1 > 3

Maggie + Matt + Josh > 3

It adds up to more than the sum of the parts. Each one could have done something on their own but because they did it together it increased the sum exponentially.

The more Matt and Maggie and I talked, the more Side Effects the book project had--on all of them.

Here are a few highlights from our conversation.

"They want it to be funny."

— Josh (letting his parents know what elementary-aged kids want to read)

"It really brought us closer together and continues to bring us closer together as a family."

— Maggie

"The vast majority of the work we did on the book was on super long drives to my mom's house. We would just bring 10 or 12 chapters of the book and read them aloud. Josh would comment on it. 12 hours go by pretty quick. Our son stays engaged for 12 hours."

— Matt

"An 11-year-old boy getting to tell his 48-year-old dad how it is."

— Matt

If you'd like to read more about their adventures in fiction, come on over to spark.repossible.com and see how they mix baseball, physics, and "Strxia, a parallel world facing certain ruin."

PART III
WHAT

"If we knew what it was we were doing, it would not be called research, would it?"

— Albert Einstein

INTRODUCTION: FIRE

"In everyone's life, at some time, our inner fire goes out. It is then burst into flame by an encounter with another human being. We should all be thankful for those people who rekindle the inner spirit."

— ALBERT SCHWEITZER

ou'd think the "What" section of this book would be simple. Here goes one option:
What are we creating here:

1. A book
2. A workshop
3. A short story
4. A cookbook
5. A song

Etc.

Although I don't disagree with the above list, it's not what I'm after. Yes, those are the "things" we're making, but I'm going to go cliché and use, "It's the journey, not the destination."

Here's a list that's a little harder to, well, hold in your hand:

1. Experience
2. Creating (better: co-creating)
3. Experiment
4. Memories
5. Time capsule
6. Love

I'm going to go out on a limb and create a quote that sums it up for me:

"Love is the overlap of the experience of two people."

- Person one can have an experience.
- Person two can have an experience.

But when person one and person two have that experience together, it's different.

- Yellow on its own is yellow.
- Green on its own is green.

But the overlap, the Venn diagram of those two elements interacting with each other becomes something different: blue.

Person one didn't have blue. Person two didn't have blue. But together, they made blue.

Yes, we'll write a book or compose a song. Great. But what I'm after is the experience of creating it together. It's not the same as two people creating separately. Yellow would still be yellow and green still green. Only together can they create blue.

Maybe it's a stretch, but what I see as the outcome or the result or benefit or side effect of Spark is, quite simply, love.

Love from one person needs love from another person to create love for each other.

I'm not talking about "I love you" and "I care about that person."

This is experience together. Working together towards a goal, finishing that goal, relishing in the success (and failures!) of the process.

Call me crazy, but that's what I call love.

You can still call me crazy.

But I have the recipe for love.

12

IT'S AN EXPERIMENT
WE CAN'T FAIL

"We often say that the biggest job we have is to teach a newly hired employee to fail intelligently... to experiment over and over again and to keep on trying and failing until he learns what will work."

— CHARLES KETTERING

*I*f we were to call this thing we're doing with the kids a test, then we'd have two probable outcomes:

- Success
- Failure

Which is why we're not going to call it a test. Or a project. Experiment.

Author's Note: I usually regret writing "Author's Note" as I'm often trying to explain something or more often making some excuse for why something isn't the way it was maybe going to be. But for the longest time, I was calling these things we're doing with our kids "projects."

What happened was that it quickly went to the dreaded *Science*

Project at school that no one wanted to do: not the parent, not the child, not even really so much the science teacher.

Except for those projects that were unexpected or unknown. They maybe didn't follow the guidelines quite right. Or they forgot to read the instructions at all. It turned from a project to an experiment.

13

THE GREAT UNKNOWN

EXPERIMENT: NOUN: AN ACT OR OPERATION FOR THE PURPOSE OF DISCOVERING SOMETHING UNKNOWN

"Experiments rarely turn out the way they're supposed to. That's why they're called experiments."

— Dawson Church

Here's how things might go:

1. You read this book,
2. You write a short book together with your 9-year-old daughter,
3. She discovers she has a talent for drawing maps and something of a sixth sense for history,
4. The UN happens to stumble upon your book (about maps and dragonflies),
5. They hire her (you, dear parent, get to tag along) to come to the former Yugoslavia to redraw the borders that will reallocate the land among Croatia and Slovenia,
6. She has a job waiting for her when she turns 16 at the UN and until then is named honorary cartographer extraordinaire.

It could happen. But this could also happen.

1. You read this book,
2. You write a short book together with your 8-year-old son,
3. It turns out, as much as I'm a fan of tortilla chips, he absolutely can't stand tortilla chips,
4. This goes so far as to stop the entire book adventure and instead you create a recipe for corn-free tortilla chips that taste just how he likes them (you're looking into a patent),
5. You write it out and take a photo of the new chip,
6. Uncle Ray at Thanksgiving said the newly-invented chip was, "Pretty good."
7. Your son is proud.
8. You are proud that your son is proud.
9. Nothing more is ever said about it again.
10. Until he's 32.

That might happen, too.

That's just it. I have no idea what's going to happen. But here's what's going to happen with inaction.

1. You don't do anything.
2. Nothing happens.

That's another option.

This is the usual option. 4 out of 5 dentists usually recommend this option. I'm trying not to say that one is better than another. They're just different.

It's an experiment. We don't know the outcome.

That's usually a good thing.

4 out of 5 times.

14

CRAIG

IT WAS KIND OF ON A WHIM.

"Where words fail, music speaks."

— Hans Christian Andersen

I'm transcribing here snippets from Craig because I can't describe his story any better than he did. Here he is:

"I'm big into meditation and I'm big into raising kids consciously and I thought, 'One day I'm going to sit down and write a simple kids' meditation.'"

"I sat down and wrote and I'm not really a writer but you can tell when something is flowing and it did. 20 minutes later I had this little script and I ran it by Emily and I ran it by my wife. There was very little editing. As a test, I thought I would have Emily just record the narration so I turned the microphone on and she recorded it and it seemed fitting."

"It was one of those projects that came together very very quickly. It still needs a little refining maybe, but that's the beauty of it, it was quick and easy and simple."

I need to stop Craig right there.

In one sentence, in fact, in 5 words, he put together 3 words that are rarely seen in the wild in the same savannah on a safari of creative projects with kids:

1. Quick
2. Easy
3. Simple

Sure, fine, 1 of the 3 we see all the time. Maybe 2 of the 3 we have together on a good day. But all three? This is like the lion and the elephant and the rhinoceros are all hanging out at the watering hole long enough for you to adjust the zoom on your brand-new camera you bought for safari.

In other words, it just doesn't happen.

But then with Craig and his daughter Emily, that's exactly what happened.

I add Craig's story here because I'd like to document, for the record, that those 3 words can be possible, that they can happen at the same time with a project with your kids. In case you're still on the floor reeling from those 3 words together about a project with your kids, I'll put them here again:

1. Quick
2. Easy
3. Simple

In case you're wondering what might come to mind when I think about creating "The Secret of Kite Hill," there are, ahem, other descriptive terms that might come up. Oh, I don't know:

1. Torture by literature
2. Bribery with salty potato products
3. Imagination chaos on a school night

No, really. Those were off the top of my head. We need to get back to Craig and Emily.

> "Encouraged her to be a part of the creative process, to do some editing, to share some opinions, and I think that helped. It wasn't me telling her what to do every step of the way. I treated her like an equal co-creator in the process and she was."

Emily was a co-creator in the process. Her dad asked for and valued her opinions. She was an integral part of it all.

> "I just asked for help, asked for her insights."

> "It's confidence building and shows that you have respect for their opinions and insights."

> "I haven't had a lot of people listen to it yet."

I've listened to the meditation called "The Wishing Well" and it's beautiful. For more about Craig, Emily, and their music, come on over to the savannah at spark.repossible.com.

15

CREATE MORE THAN YOU CONSUME
MOST PEOPLE ARE PASSIVE. THEY TAKE INFORMATION IN.

"One of the characteristics common to best-selling authors is a focus on creation. They are much more interested in producing information than consuming it."

— Dawson Church

Have you ever noticed there aren't too many books for children on how to ride a bike?

While travel books can "make it almost like you're really there," you're not really there.

How about a study course for babies on how to walk? Complete with diagrams, charts, and a table that parents can fill in with progress.

TIP: babies can't read.

BONUS TIP: babies don't need a book to teach them how to walk, they just need to try, fall down, learn, and try again.

The book you're holding in your hands is my 14th book. Let's do a little math. What is 14 minus 14? Zero! Excellent. Book number one took me 36 years to write. Book number two took another 10 years.

When people ask me how I come up with the ideas on what to write about then I know they're not creators. I have too many ideas. I have so many words. I have descriptions and scenes and philosophies and topics I don't know much about but can't wait to learn about so I read and watch and then to really learn: I write.

To use the quote above and apply it to myself:

I am much more interested in producing information than consuming it.

This part is where the physics gets a little difficult to explain, but by creating, I am actually "getting" more than I am "giving."

By doing, I am learning more than reading or watching or listening to someone telling me to do.

Yet, here we are, here I am going on and on about doing and creating and writing and you're reading.

I can't write your book for you. I can't paint your painting or create your recipe or compose your song. Well, yes, of course I could, but that's not the point. The point is for you to do, to make, to build, to write, to create.

Because let's face the cold, hard facts: there is no substitute.

- Through creating, I am learning.
- By creating, I am giving.
- By creating, I am receiving more than I am giving.

I'm not suggesting we all become prolific creators who…OK, fine, that's exactly what I'm suggesting.

If there are "secrets" in this book that I wish to convey only to those who read it through and through, this is one of them: create.

- Consuming is passive
- Creating is active

If you read this book and think about creating an experiment with your kid it's like reading the manual on riding a bike. There is no substitute for experience.

Most people are passive. They take information in.

We can't change the past. We can create our present reality. By creating our present, we are setting the trajectory of our future.

Yes, I have a book planned called: Create.

Because it's just that important.

16

ARLENE
THAT MEAN GIRL THING

"When you're nice, you're not bullying people. But when you're kind, you stand up against the bully."

— Daniel Lubetzky

"*...A* journey of self discovery using NLP, Hypnotherapy, Magic, and Meditation."

Do you ever have it where your kid's school has a program or an event but it sounds so good you'd like to do it yourself? I had this with one of the high schools we looked at for my son because it had a sport program that included surfing for a week in Spain. Then I had it with what Arlene did together with her daughters.

"I didn't want to just talk to them anymore, it wasn't making a difference. I wanted to model it for them, teach the girls tools they could use. Really and truly, my intention was for them to come to know that they were powerful and indeed magic."

Arlene's two young girls (7 and 9) were being bullied at school-- even by friends.

"I wanted to create something with the girls using the stories they told me to help to empower them."

She tried to get girls together to work through a program. At her first attempt to get girls' parents on board, they all said no.

She looked further. Found other girls, other parents. With the new group of girls, she asked them what they wanted from the workshop.

- Gained Confidence
- Finding their voice
- Healthy Relationships and Positive Lifestyle
- Support for the development of leadership and life skills
- Sense of belonging or connected
- Increased Community Connections
- Encourage the awareness of their core values, personal interests, strengths and attributes, and above all, knowing that they were magic.

Who wouldn't want all that? Now the parents were on board when they saw the list.

To this point, I remind us all to know our own goals of our experiment. My own simple goal back in 2014 was to write a book in a month and get it on Amazon. Simple goal, deadline, done.

Arlene has loftier yet still very accomplish-able goals and that helped get the parents to believe in what she was doing--and it helps us and the kids, too.

"Building the program was easy, having them participate in the program was my challenge. It was easy to get the buy in from the parents. I simply gave them the list up above, but getting the buy in from the girls proved to be difficult at times."

Sure, the list above was great to convince that parents that this whole endeavor was a good idea. But how to get the kids involved?

"We worked together from week to week, and at points and time, one would project onto the other, or onto themselves. There were times when I had to leave one child for alone time, to simply feel what they were feeling and held the space for what came up. What I discovered while running this program was that they absolutely loved the magic.

Each week I would incorporate a nature walk. We would feel the trees and the different energy of the trees, and then I would would have them tune into each other, to feel how each person had a unique signature. One week we played in a field, I had one girl on her own at the end of one field, facing away from the group. She would keep her eyes closed, building upon the energy work we had taught in prior weeks, I had the girls ground their energy and create a bubble of their energy around them. Then one by one a child would step forward towards the girl facing the other direction. The girl with her back turned was instructed to come name who was coming towards her as soon as she felt them.

The results were amazing. 3 of the 5 girls were 100%, while I could see the two girls who guessed incorrectly, second guessed their intuition just before saying the name. As awesome as this was, it created a sense of comparison between them all. And though my intention was to empower, the two girls closed themselves off for the rest of the class."

What I'm proposing in Spark is an experiment. An experiment means we're testing, trying, playing. It's not perfect yet and maybe never needs to be. What works we can do more of. What doesn't work we can do less of.

Arlene continued learning, revamping, and playing.

"There were great learnings in this program that I would incorporate into others, it was a 2 steps forward, 1 step back full of insights about how they saw themselves.

My own daughter sat out some of the time, and no matter what I did, she would not join the group. I simply had to work with what I had.

Would I do this again? Absolutely!

In following up with the girls, they've all forgotten their tools... so one key next step is, how do I maintain and empower the girls so that they are inspired to continue using them? I ran this program 2 years ago and when I see most of the girls, they'd love for me to run it again. One child can't seem to look me in the eyes, such a curious thing and regardless, I just might run the program this summer, make it bigger and better.

There's nothing like being reminded of the magic within.

Empowered with tools and skills, reminded of your uniqueness and playing outside under the sun."

Magic? Outdoors? Empowerment? What could go wrong? What could go right?

When I first started this project, I had two quick ideas:

1. Bradley writes book with kids and shares experiences and instructions on how others can do it too.
2. Bradley's story is OK. We need other stories that are not about 2 boys and a book.

What I like about Arlene's story is that I never would have thought of it. That's what makes it different and new and exciting.

If you'd like to hear more about Arlene's story and her plans for more "I'm IN" workshops, join us over at spark.repossible.com.

PART IV
WHEN

"It was like there was a pile of kindling that was in the back of my imagination just waiting there. Once I lit it, it just flared up and I kept getting ideas and ideas."

— Kevin J. Anderson

INTRODUCTION: KINDLING

"The best time to plant a tree was 20 years ago. The second best time is now."

— CHINESE PROVERB

My dad passed away in 2015. I struggle sometimes to understand the idea in time that he'll never come back. The idea of never being the word I can't really comprehend.

In 2014, my boys were 8 and 10 when we "did that book project" as they like to refer to it. Never again will Lu (admittedly and voluntarily) write a little story about farting and aliens.

There is no way I could now get my 15-year-old-hair-in-his-armpits son Li to sit down a record a chapter of a book he wrote and follow through with it until it was right.

But frankly, I got what I wanted. What I have today is the audio of each boy reading their own chapters. It's priceless. Of all of the Side Effects and Benefits of this entire operation, those two audio files are what I cherish most.

They'll never be 8 and 10 again. In fact, it was only during that year.

This section is called When. For me, the answer to that question is simple: now.

Or to put it even more strongly: It's now or never.

I smell a chapter title...

18

IT'S NOW OR NEVER
PLEASE DON'T WAIT 12 YEARS

"Every now and then a man's mind is stretched by a new idea or sensation, and never shrinks back to its former dimensions."

— Oliver Wendell Holmes, Jr.

*1*2 years from now will be too late.
Seth Godin has a habit of writing a few sentences that hit home. Did I mention he writes Every Single Day? What a concept. Here's Seth:

> "Twelve years from now, your future self is going to thank you for something you did today, for an asset you began to build, a habit you formed, a seed you planted. Even if you're not sure of where it will lead, today's the day to begin."
>
> — Seth Godin

I waited 10 years. Here's a quick timeline of my early author career:

1. 2004: wrote a book,
2. 2014: wrote next book.

What happened in between? Easy: nothing--at least not as far as my dream of writing books. Did you do the math there? 2014 - 2004 = 10. Those are years. I can't get those back.

What's most interesting about Seth's post is this part:
your *future self* is going to thank (the *present) you*
We're not talking about:

- The press,
- The Oscars,
- Your kids,
- Your spouse,
- Your fans,
- Your worldwide tour promoter.

We're talking about:

1. Your future self
2. thanking you (that is, your present self).

It's so simple. So powerful. So hard.
Yet so easy.
It begins with the first step.
What are you waiting for?
Please don't wait 12 years. Your future self will thank your current self.

∼

Flashback
Red chair. Living room. San Francisco. March 3, 2014.
Sitting with my 8-year-old son after having read a so-so

children's book, my past, present, and future passed before my eyes. I (past) had wanted to be a writer, I (present) wasn't a writer and I (future) wanted to be a writer. For some reason, it hit me that this was one of those now-or-never moments.

19

RICH
ARE CHINASAURS EXTINCT?

"The future is wide open. I may actually go back and get that law degree someday."

— Gretchen Carlson

*A*s much as I don't like the "threat" of It's Now or Never, it really comes down to...It's Now or Never.

My 15-year-old-almost-shaving son would need a large pizza, a new PS4 game, and an unlimited mobile data plan to even get near a microphone to record the audiobook version of the book we wrote.

When my kids were 8 and 10, it was Then or Never. Technically speaking, 4 years later is equivalent to never.

My partner in crime for the Markree Castle series, Rich Robinson, was busy with a project called "Chinasaurs" around the time we were working on Markree Castle.

He lives in Beijing, China, (thus the book name) and had worked together with a paleontologist and his two boys to put together a book about dinosaurs in China.

They sketched out storyboards, met with the paleontologist, and had most of an outline. They were going strong and then, somewhere along the way, from an unknown corner of the universe, timed just right to collide with their enthusiasm, youth, and efforts, life happened.

The project never got finished.

As Rich and I spoke about it, it was clear that it would most probably never get done. His boys are now older and about as interested in dinosaurs as my boys are interested in castles in Ireland.

In case that wasn't clear, think about a thing you sort of have to do but don't really truly have to do, others would like you to do it, they'd even like you to be interested in it but you're clearly not, and the only reason you might think of doing the thing is to please them, but if you're a 15-year-old-boy, that's not really in your wheelhouse.

The boys weren't too beat up about it, but Rich was.

It's also difficult to measure if the boys might have thought too much differently had they finished the project.

For pictures of Rich's boys' storyboards and the Chinasaurs project, visit spark.repossible.com.

∼

> *Flashback*
> *Bathroom Mirror, Driebergen, The Netherlands*
> *"I think I need to shave. Dad, can we buy some razors?"*
> *Just recently turned 15-year-old Li doesn't not remember Kite Hill, but mostly because it's how we walked home from school for six years. But "The Secret of Kite Hill"? Oh yeah, that book project we did together.*

20

LIZZ
WAITING FOR THE PERFECT TIME

"If you look to your past or even your present to see why you are here or what your purpose is, you may get stuck in a limited view of yourself. Instead, look beyond your years here on earth, reconnect with the divine, and bring forth your soul's legacy into the present moment."

— Debbie Ford

*L*izz would love to write a book together with her kids. She'd love to write a book at all. I'm pretty sure she'd be rather pleased with writing anything.

There are few things holding her back:

1. Reality
2. Time
3. Pressure
4. The present moment
5. Decisions
6. Excuses
7. Other stuff

We could probably narrow that down to just two:

1. Reality
2. Other stuff

"Why is Lizz a chapter of this book if she hasn't yet completed the experiment?" I hear you whispering to yourself.

She's in here exactly because she hasn't yet completed the experiment. She's here so we can root her on. So I can call her out and, yep, put her in the spotlight, and remind her (and me and us and you) that:

We're rooting for you.

My intention with this book is not to show you how fantastic we all are who created these magnificent experiments with their kids and they're now leading global initiatives.

My intention is to create.

My intention is to start with nothing and create something, together with a younger person we love. Oh, and finish it.

Lizz, you're here to lead us. We're following in your footsteps. We're rooting for you. We're behind you all the way. We want to see what you come up with.

This is an experiment. We cannot fail. There is no failure. There is only learning, experiencing, getting done, and moving on to the next adventure.

That's why Lizz gets her own chapter.

21

LORENA
WE CAN ALWAYS FINISH IT TOMORROW

"Never put off till tomorrow what you can do the day after tomorrow."

— Mark Twain

*L*orena and her son created a fantastic adventure complete with colorful characters, funny names, and a moving story of how to fit in with others when you're different.

They worked on the story together, built out the characters with even more detail, and even gave the book a title: "Kungi Kanga."

When I asked her where the story was today, the pain and regret were evident in her voice.

The story was in a file on her computer. As we talked about it more, she even went so far as to say that the characters were imprisoned within the plastic walls of her computer and have never been out to see the light of day or transformed into ink on a page of a book.

Lorena is an author who has written several books, but the one that possibly pains her the most is the one that is trapped in the prison of the past.

Although there is not yet a happy ending to this story, there could be (especially with encouragement from us, the readers of this book and participants in this adventure). The file is still on her computer. She hasn't deleted it.

In fact, the prison where this story still lives is the worst kind of prison. This kind of prison has no locks and no doors yet it's difficult to escape.

The key to setting the story free lies not in the past and not in the future but in the present. The key to bringing her son's imagination to life lies in the simple but not always easy task of taking action to finish a project started long ago.

Often the longer we wait, the more difficult it is to reinvigorate something from the past but it's still possible. Easier, as I'm sure you can imagine at this point, is to finish what we begin without delay, without unnecessary doubt, and can take a line from a child's innocent and pure playbook and ask not why the story should come to life but why not?

In this book, I almost don't dare tell you that rekindling an old project is even harder than beginning a new project because I don't want you to to be discouraged and never begin. For the most part, I believe that starting the project releases enthusiasm, confidence, and an accountability from yourself and your team to keep going.

Perhaps it's not necessarily that finishing a project is more difficult than starting a project but in terms of pain, guilt, and regret, not finishing a project is far worse than not starting.

> *Flashback*
> *Hallway, Driebergen, The Netherlands*
> *There was some old paint on a door frame. It had been there "forever." But of course it hadn't been there forever. It was maybe 6 months. Maybe it was a year. Maybe it actually was forever.*
> *But I walked by it everyday and saw it. I noticed it. I knew*

I would "someday" get a knife or one of those spatula scraper things and clean it off.

But I never did.

Until I did.

What had bugged me on a daily basis for what seemed like eternity took approximately 8 minutes to solve.

Let's do a little math, shall we?

5 seconds of annoyance x 184 days = just way too much

8 minutes to solve or wait another 5 seconds for X number of days?

Could it be that simple to fix the one-time job for a lifetime of no longer daily annoyances?

Could it be that simple?

PART V

HOW

"A person who never made a mistake never tried anything new."

— ALBERT EINSTEIN

INTRODUCTION: SPARKS

"Education is not the filling of a pail, but the lighting of a fire."

— WILLIAM BUTLER YEATS

This is the section where I explain how to do it.

I have talked with lots (no, really, way too many) of people about Spark. Often when I get into the How of it all, they'll say:

"But it's easy for you to say, you've already done it."

Let's do some more examples, just for kicks:

- The marathon runner runs marathons. (Because he's already in shape.)
- The brain surgeon does brain surgery. (He studied it and, hopefully, has had lots of experience performing brain surgeries.)
- I have written 5 books with my kids. (Because I got that first one started and done.)

Did I just put myself in a bullet list with marathon runners and brain surgeons? Absolutely.

They all had a Day One. That day when they knew nothing, couldn't do anything, were beginners.

After my MBA, I was a Management Consultant. The big secret behind management consulting is that you just need to be one step ahead (or off to the side) of the client.

We only need to be one step ahead of our kids.

"Wait. Dad. Sorry, but what did you say we were going to do in February? Did you say we're going to write a book together?"

Cue answer card: "Yes!"

See, you're already ahead of them.

Now that you're brimming with confidence, let's jump right into car repair.

23

REPLACE CAR ENGINE IN TWO STEPS
HERE'S EXACTLY HOW TO DO IT

"Everything from airplanes to kitchen blenders and even chopsticks comes with an instruction manual. Children, despite all their complexity, do not."

— Lawrence Kutner

I was a huge fan of the "Car Talk" radio show. Two brothers who were car mechanics talked about car repair. I'm not a car guy. You'd think, "Bradley, why in the world would you listen to a radio show about car repair?"

It was basically a comedy hour. The two guys were so funny it didn't matter what they were talking about.

One of my favorite pieces was when they explained how to replace a car engine. It was a perfect example of Simple But Not Easy. I'll let you in on their secret instruction manual.

How to replace a car engine:

1. Remove old engine.
2. Drop in new engine.

There you have it. It's not wrong. But it also doesn't really give you many details.

Here you go. Now that we're deep into this book, I'm just going to go ahead and give you the:

Instruction Manual to write a book with your kids

1. Find kid.
2. Write a book together.

There you have it. We're done! Simple. But not necessarily easy.

We also don't need to go to the gym. Seriously, what do you call those conveyor belts to run on? What, is the pavement outside broken? Put on shoes. Go outside. Move legs. Return home at some point.

Kids don't read instruction manuals to learn how to ride a bike. They hop on, crash, and do better the next time. Soon, they get it.

It's that simple.

No, really. It is.

I can (and will be happy to) give you all kinds of instructions and tips and tricks, tactics and strategies, and dive deep into the case studies of my own kids and those who have granted access to the stories of their own adventures in this book, but it's going to come down to you and a kid and writing a book (or painting a canvas or composing a song or whatever).

Just in case you're searching in this book for How To Do It, I'll put it down here again:

1. Find kid.
2. Write a book together.

Here, this will help: a deadline.

Let's move on to the next chapter.

24

HALFWAY WILL NEVER FINISH
IT WILL BE DONE BY THE END OF THE MONTH

"The best thing for my creative process is a deadline."

— Jeff MacNelly

I specifically remember a math word problem in school in which one of the race contestants would get halfway to the finish line with each effort. At the beginning, he was way out in front. With one step, he'd gone halfway to the finish line.

The trick, the joke, the bad news comes when you realize that halfway will never get to the finish line. Sure, at the end, the distance will be microscopic, but by definition, he'll never make it.

It doesn't matter how fast you're out of the starting gate or even how quick your pace is.

We want to finish this thing.

The only thing that works for me is a deadline. We have one: the last day of the month.

There, problem solved.

25

CREATE A CONFLICT
YOUR CHILD WILL FIND A WAY TO SOLVE IT

"Every problem has in it the seeds of its own solution. If you don't have any problems, you don't get any seeds."

— Norman Vincent Peale

I know, I know. I can hear you.

"Hey, that's really cute about the car engine and everything, but I honest and truly don't know where to start."

I get it.

Keep in mind this doesn't need to be a book. But for the sake of simplicity and because I'm the one with the keyboard (at least in this chapter), I'm going to give you the inside scoop on how to write a book with your kids.

Houston, we need a problem.

Kids are remarkably imaginative. Take that glowing device out of their hands for a few minutes and brain cells rejoice and start forming new synapses and connections and are partying like it's 1999.

But they need a challenge. A question. Somewhere to start.

What can you take from your everyday life to stir up a little pandemonium? What can you (at least for the sake of literary beginnings) take away from your child they'll miss dearly? Start with that.

I tend to think in book titles. Here are a few that would rattle my sons:

1. The Perilous Adventure of How Lu Beat Li in 1-on-1 Basketball
2. Is that Dog Barf on my Waffle?
3. Why Lu is So Much Better than Li (Book 1 of the 274-book series written solely by Lu)
4. How My Job at Foot Locker Rocketed My Entrepreneurial Success (clearly non-fiction)
5. The Thanksgiving when I Pulled the Wart off of Aunt Hildegard's Nose
6. New Year's Eve Fireworks Laws (and how to avoid them)

Are these triggering anything? Firing up some really bad story about your cousin and his visit over the holidays?

Here are a few other tried and true tactics:

1. What if you wrote a book that no one would ever see? (except maybe mom)
2. Shoot for the worst book of fiction known to the history of literature--and the shortest.
3. The secret book that only you and your kid knew about.
4. Write a 4-page book with no verbs.
5. Let your child tell a story where your only question is, "Then what happened?" (Keep at it until he falls over or needs food.)

Maybe a non-fiction book would delight your little know-it-all. What are they good at? How could they help someone else with their knowledge? What "How To" book might they write?

Or they might want to jump into research because they want their book to be better and they realize at some point that no, they don't actually know everything and that others know some other things and if they talk to them they might learn something--and can put it in their book and their book will be better, more interesting, and might even develop into a different book.

Gee, where could I have ever heard of this concept?

Or maybe it's fiction and storytelling for your child. I don't know about you, but if I started off with "The Thanksgiving when I Pulled the Wart off of Aunt Hildegard's Nose" to a kid and let them tell me the story, I think I'd be in for a rollicking ride of imagination.

For more ideas, questions, and starting blocks, come on over and join Camp Spark at spark.repossible.com.

26

MEG
ELEMENTAL P

"The future belongs to those who believe in the beauty of their dreams."

— Eleanor Roosevelt

If you grew up in the United States (and maybe other English-speaking countries, let me know if you recognize this...), you learn the alphabet by a song made up of all 26 letters. Well, a "song" might be a big word. It's just a sing-song melody of the letters but as soon as anyone who recognizes the tune they'll jump in and finish.

When Meg was 5 years old, she thought the part where they spell out "L M N O P" was actually "Elemental P."

Here's Meg with the play by play of how it went down.

"It's all stick figures. I did the broad strokes on the figures but he did all of the outfits on them. He's very much into clothes and designing. They all have pretty elaborate outfits on them.

We give the books away at schools and the kids are mesmerized by Matthew. Authors are a big deal. Every time they read a book, they learn about authors, they know about authors, they read authors in a series. Matthew is in 3rd grade now. They're blown away.

He was in kindergarten when we wrote it. He was in 1st grade when we finally got it published.

He's creative. I'm not particularly creative. I'm a lawyer.

Of course he wants to write another one.

He loved books. I read probably 4 books to him per night from the time he was 6 months old.

It's good. Kids like it. They really respond to it. It's all educational. He insists on personally handing out every book to every kid.

The first one he was nervous and now he's all in."

On the back cover of the book, Meg thanks her mother (Matthew's grandmother) "for believing in our dream and helping to make it come true."

It turns out, this adventure, this experiment is not always just about the two of you. It might extend beyond your household and touch and involve and even need the support of those around you.

A father of one of Matthew's classmates helped out with printing. Another friend connected with an author for advice.

It didn't start our simple and easy. But it became both. Together with people who came to them to help, who were inspired by what they were doing, they made it happen.

It became bigger than just the two of them. It became bigger than 1 + 1. It was their experiment together.

27

WANT TO TRULY LEARN SOMETHING? LEARN IT THROUGH YOUR KIDS.

I WAS PRETTY SURE I KNEW EVERYTHING. TURNS OUT I KNEW NOTHING.

"If you're not making mistakes, then you're not doing anything. I'm positive that a doer makes mistakes."

— John Wooden

You think you know about a topic? See what your kids learn during a (school) project then compare that with what you thought you knew.

Learn through what your kids learn.

Don't read the article or the book yourself and come to your own conclusions.

1. Read the article (or sections of a book) **aloud** to your kids and then do not give them your opinion.
2. **Listen** to their first comments.
3. **Ask** further questions. (Still not giving your opinion.)
4. Allow the awkward **silence**. Listen to what they have to say about it when you don't talk about it.

You're learning about the topic, but you're also learning how your child is learning.

1. What did they pick up from what you read?
2. Was it anything close to what you got out of it?
3. Did they pick up important details?
4. Did they miss something important?
5. Were they listening at all?

This is a good way to see how much comprehension they actually have from content.

John Wooden

Famed UCLA Basketball coach John Wooden didn't like being called "The Wizard of Westwood" as he mentions below (see quotes) because a wizard was seen as "being some sort of magician" and to the contrary, he believed deeply in hard work, making mistakes, and sweating the details.

He didn't like being call a wizard, but we could at least call him a wise philosopher.

I consciously added this chapter to the book partly because it was a learning experience through doing a project together with my son but also because John Wooden has been a hero of mine since I was a kid and I'm proud to feature him anywhere I possibly can.

Share the quotes below with your child and see if any of them resonate.

John Wooden Quotes

1. If you're not making mistakes, then you're not doing anything. I'm positive that a doer makes mistakes.
2. I'm no wizard, and I don't like being thought of in that light at all. I think of a wizard as being some sort of

magician or something, doing something on the sly or something, and I don't want to be thought of in that way.
3. Whatever you do in life, surround yourself with smart people who'll argue with you.
4. It's the little details that are vital. Little things make big things happen.
5. Be true to yourself, help others, make each day your masterpiece, make friendship a fine art, drink deeply from good books – especially the Bible, build a shelter against a rainy day, give thanks for your blessings and pray for guidance every day.
6. Things turn out best for the people who make the best of the way things turn out.
7. I think the teaching profession contributes more to the future of our society than any other single profession.
8. Be more concerned with your character than your reputation, because your character is what you really are, while your reputation is merely what others think you are.
9. The most important thing in the world is family and love.
10. Do not let what you cannot do interfere with what you can do.
11. It isn't what you do, but how you do it.
12. Today is the only day. Yesterday is gone.
13. Don't give up on your dreams, or your dreams will give up on you.
14. The main ingredient of stardom is the rest of the team.
15. Well, your greatest joy definitely comes from doing something for another, especially when it was done with no thought of something in return.
16. You can't live a perfect day without doing something for someone who will never be able to repay you.
17. If I am through learning, I am through.
18. Failure is never fatal. But failure to change can and might be.

Flashback

Kitchen table. Learn from the student.

Then 9-year old Lu did a school project on John Wooden. I thought I knew Coach Wooden pretty well. I even have a signed copy of "Practical Modern Basketball" I got signed by Coach Wooden in person while at a UCLA game maybe around the time I was...9-years old. Of course, I never actually read the book. Turns out I had a lot to learn. About John Wooden. And about learning. I learned more in the short time with Lu and his school project than I had in a lifetime of following the great coach—and not actually reading what he wrote.

Bonus Exercise

I must add this in here as it worked wonders, is oddly easy, and is fun at the same time.

Can't get your kids to do their homework? Turn on the time-lapse video option and let your kid know he's the star and everything he does is being recorded.

Keep it on until they finish their homework. Let them watch it when they're done. I'll make sure I have the video of my son working on his John Wooden report at spark.repossible.com.

Come check it out and if you do one, share yours with us too.

28

HOW TO MAKE FRIENDS AND INFLUENCE...YOUR KIDS
LET'S BRING IN SOME TRIED-AND-TRUE MANAGEMENT TECHNIQUES

"Don't worry that children never listen to you; worry that they are always watching you."

— Robert Fulghum

When you're working with kids (or, for that matter, adults who act like kids), there are some project management techniques that can be extremely helpful, time saving, and fun.

Fun?

I needed the boys to answer a few questions about their characters in the Kite Hill book. Fun stuff: character traits, magical powers, and "catch phrase."

> *Author's note: this was written when we were working on The Markree Castle series. I'm going to leave it in the present tense from then as it gives the authentic feel of what I was doing at the time.*
>
> *Doctor's note: I think the boys are a little obsessed with In-*

N-Out Burger. You might want to look into talking with a nutritionist.

1.) Don't edit

As expected, my older son jumped right in. "I know, I know," he said, almost shaking as he couldn't wait to get it out. "I'd have a magic straw that was white and red and when I waved it, I could have any In-N-Out order I wanted!" He waved his invisible wand, "A Double Double!" Waved again, "A vanilla shake!" I think he was hungry…I did pick them up a little late.

Later I learned that he meant that the straw/wand created an actual In-N-Out building! Glad I didn't understand at the time as I liked the visual of the cheeseburger and shake appearing in the forest of Ireland quite magically culinary.

2.) Be enthusiastic about their answers

I didn't have to fake it: I laughed hard and out loud at the In-N-Out magical power. You always think they'll go for flying or invisible cloaks or potions. But the whole vision of In-N-Out was priceless. Enthusiasm? Check!

3.) Listen

Comment on their answers that show you're listening.

"I bet your buddies Dec & Den are going to LOVE your In-N-Out wand!" I said without hesitation or exaggeration.

Dec & Den are their friends who are going to be sharing the pages of adventure in their upcoming book based on a weekend of adventures in a castle in Ireland. "So," I asked in all seriousness … wow, maybe I was hungry too … "Can your wand make In-N-Out appear for everyone or just you?"

"For anyone," he said. Oh goodie.

4.) Keep the momentum

If there are less fun questions, sneak those in while the iron is hot. I wanted to gather some "character traits" (e.g. shy, silly, honest, etc.), but wasn't sure how to ask. So I just asked. I got the answers (older boy said, "Honest, good at American football.") and moved on.

5.) Listen

No, it's not a typo. If you can listen (and then listen some more), you've already leaped out of the starting gates.

29

BRAD

WHAT DO YOU THINK ABOUT YOUR DAD?

"I was not naturally talented. I didn't sing, dance or act, though working around that minor detail made me inventive."

— Steve Martin

Brad was just asking for trouble.
Oh, I know, here's a way to challenge the universe as we know it:

1. Set up a camera,
2. Turn it on,
3. Sit with your daughter (or any available child),
4. Ask them questions. Like an interview.
5. You could ask "safe" questions like, "What does Christmas mean to you?" or "In general, do you think teenagers are dumb?"
6. Or you could invite immediate danger and ask them things like, "What do you think of your dad?"
7. Let them speak,
8. Hear them out,

9. Be patient,
10. Listen,
11. Post it on YouTube.

I was good with it all up to #11. He's asking for it.

But this is exactly what he did.

He turned his sons and daughters into actors, performers, and interviewees. Just like that. With a camera. Turned on.

He transformed what might have been "an interesting conversation" that in all probability never would have been remembered by either party involved, into a time capsule of a moment of dad at that time and daughter at that time.

He has different videos of his kids at different times with different topics. I think it would be a neat project to do every year and see how the kids (and the adults) progressed (or digressed...). But I'm getting ahead of myself.

Here you go, here's an easy one (full of potential downside and upside). Just make one video together with your kids.

1. Hit record on your phone,
2. Ask them one question,
3. Listen.

You don't have to post it on YouTube.

Need some questions? I bet Brad has some for us. See his nail-biting cliffhangers over at spark.repossible.com and we'll rustle up some safe questions to ask your kids in an "interview."

Then we'll get to some you only have to ask if you're a daredevil, risk taker, and rockstar. Like Brad.

30
DON'T TALK ABOUT THE PROJECT. START THE PROJECT.
JUMP RIGHT IN.

"In Missouri, where I come from, we don't talk about what we do—we just do it. If we talk about it, it's seen as bragging."

— Brad Pitt

There are a few schools of thought on this topic. Let's try to get them squared away so you know what works best for you.

I'm talking about two different things here:

1. Telling your kids about what you're doing,
2. Telling friends, family, coworkers, and strangers about what you're doing.

We'll make sure to cover both. My main philosophy here is: whatever works.

1.) Tell no one

Kids

The Ideal World. Depending the ages of the kids, this could go both ways. We all hope the kids will be enthusiastic about joining the family endeavor so tell them, have them involved from the start.

Reality Teen Drama. If I so much as mention "work" or "project" to any male young person above the age of, say, 12, they might win the Olympic relay and run away with...the TV remote. I often resorted to underhanded, sleight-of-hand trickery to get to the next stage of our undertaking.

Adults

Have you ever opened up to a friend about something and regretted it the minute they had their first reaction? If you'd like to keep things safe for a while, don't tell anyone what you're doing. If the entire enterprise turns into the biggest disaster in the history of your family, no harm done--and even your family will laugh about it later. Well, maybe much later.

2.) Tell a select few

Kids

Make it a select, exclusive, members-only crew of highly sought out individuals. OK, so even if it's not that, you can easily make it sound like that.

Adults

With the right group, you'll get enthusiastic folks cheering you on and those who don't know won't be bothered by it. If you do this right, you might even pique the interest of those you thought would never be interested. Win win.

3.) Tell everyone

Kids

Go overboard. Tell your kids. Tell their friends. Be overly, annoyingly enthusiastic to the point where your kids will forcibly hold you back from talking about "The Thing We're Doing." This can be lots of fun and get more and more people involved.

Adults

If you're the type who announces, "I'm going to lose 2 pounds by January 31!" and then you actually do it, you might be better off telling everyone this is what you're doing.

Flashback
Corbett Street, San Francisco, Mistake #1
I made the first mistake about talking about "The Book Project" while walking home from school. I quickly changed the subject to something completely different when I got not-exactly-jumping-for-joy responses and remembered this rule: don't talk about what you're going to do, just get started and let them be a part of it. If you're savvy, you'll get them to even want to help. Sound impossible? Very Tom Sawyer and white picket fences, I know.

31

KEEP IT LEGAL, BUT KEEP IT REAL
IT'S SORT OF LIKE COOPERATION, BUT IT'S OCCASIONALLY COMPETITION.

"My parents are very competitive, so we are very competitive as kids. But it's a good kind of competition; it's not a jealousy. You always want to do your best, and if it can't be you, you want it to be your brother or your sister, you know what I mean?"

— Janet Jackson

There might possibly be times, now and again, few and far between, roughly on the schedule of the lunar eclipse, or maybe a meteor shower, where you might need to bring in the big guns, the hired hands, the friends at the table.

Let's take a trip back to the pasta restaurant off Highway 80.

> *Flashback*
> *Spaghetti Factory. Rancho Cordova, California.*
> *I wasn't getting any answers. I wasn't even getting responses. I'm not sure there was a pulse. It was time to call in the big boys. Or at least, the other boys.*
> *I looked over at Li and Lu's friends sitting at our same table.*
> *"So Aiden, say there's a good guy working at a castle and*

> then there's a bad guy also working at a castle. How are they related?"
>
> Zero bites of spaghetti and 10 minutes later, I had the next chapter (and an underlying fight for power over the castle) from Li's friend.
>
> Aiden went back to his spaghetti, I furiously took notes on a napkin, and my boys woke up and wanted in on the action.
>
> My kids weren't providing the goods. It was clearly time to outsource.

Let's have a quick look at what transpired among the gluten-free pasta with Mizithra cheese and brown butter.

We had a deadline. I was a bit stuck. I needed a fresh perspective on the conflict between the good guy and the bad guy in the Markree Castle series. I asked my team. They were sick of me and much more interested in the bottomless iced tea.

Sure, I could build this up and use big words like:

- Coercion
- Jealousy
- Envy
- FOMO

But let's keep it friendly among friends (and meatballs). Here's the real shining gem in the rough: Aiden was into it. I couldn't even keep up with his imagination and storyline that he just kept building and growing. He was getting more and more into it.

He was having a blast.

See what happened there?

Here I am working on my own kids and *trying* to get them to participate when the boy across the table is *willing* and *able*.

Let's do a quick round up of the table scorecard:

- Able? 4

- Able but not willing? 3
- Not able and not willing? 0
- Able and willing? 1

Work with what you have on hand

My older son is quickly envious of my younger son, so I figured if I could get the younger one involved, the older one would want to be a part of it. I needed the answer from Li, but he wasn't talking.

I asked my younger son the question, "If you could have any magical power, what would it be?"

It's a fun question to be sure, and my younger son went straight into creative imagination mode.

"I could create 'Mini Me' creatures whenever I wanted to. Each little version of me would have a gatling gun and..."

OK, he qualifies for being 100% boy as most creative explorations involve guns, explosions, farts or butts. Better yet if they include all them.

Now that Lu answered and Li was probably simmering with all kinds of imaginative ideas, Li finally answered.

The direct question didn't work. However, the indirect "jealousy" trick worked wonders.

Keep it legal, but keep it real.

32

LINDA
WHAT DO YOU, THE PARENT, LOVE TO DO?

"Writing, film, sculpture, music: it's all make-believe, really."

— Kate Bush

*L*inda is a musician. She said:

"Music has always been a huge part of my life."

Both she and her husband are in bands. Their children, when they were born, were not born musicians. The parents brought to the children what was close to them, what they were good at, what they loved.

For her father's 80th birthday, they created a parody of a song and performed it. Here's Linda in her own words and my bumbling.

> Me: "You created something. You made this song, you wrote it together in the car on the way there. You performed it with your family for your dad."
>
> Linda: "Yeah."

Me: "Wow."

Me: "You could have all chipped in and got him a chainsaw for his birthday. Some item. Some thing at the store. You created something from nothing. You created a song, there was no song. You did this thing and you gave it to him."

Linda: "It was somewhat conscious. It was something we always thought was so fun. It was always so well received. It was a very satisfying creative process."

Me: "Mom and dad do these parodies, it looks like fun. That's really neat that you do that. But what you did was you brought the kids in and said, 'Hey, not only do mom and dad do this but we're going to bring the kids in and do this together.' You involved them."

Sure, maybe if you're a hired assassin or an astronaut, it might be a little harder to share What You Do and Love with your kids.

But if you're stuck at the point of, "Gee, I'm not creative." or "I don't know what we'd do together." then maybe letting them into a part of your world is an idea.

Not that they have to study the 7-volume "Corporate Tax Law in New York State (updated 2014)" with you, but how could you give them a tiny little glimpse into something you love?

PART VI

CAMPFIRE STORIES

"Life is an adventure, it's not a package tour."

— Eckhart Tolle

33

INTRODUCTION: MATCHES

"We've had bad luck with our kids—they've all grown up."

— Christopher Morley

I suppose if I'm going to keep going with the whole fire and spark and camping metaphor, I need to keep it going even all the way down here in Part 6.

I've been working on this book for the past four years.

Ever since we wrote some of the first lines of "The Secret of Kite Hill" and I mentioned to anyone (parents or not) what I was doing, there was a reaction. A strong reaction. An emotional reaction. Let's see if I can bring some of them back:

- **Insanity:** "I'm sorry, did you say you're doing this willingly or is this part of your parole violation agreement?"
- **Love:** "That's the most beautiful thing I've ever heard. Your kids are going to thank you someday for this from the bottom of their hearts." (Author's note: I'm not holding my breath, but I think it might arrive before the year 2034.)

- **Guilt:** "Wow, I'm not sure I know my middle daughter's middle name."
- **Cooperation:** "Dude, tell me when you're ready for the next one, I'd love to be a part of it."

Part of the reason I enjoy writing books is because it's an adventure, an experiment, and it helps define who I am for that period in my life.

I don't just write books. I live them.

I talk to random strangers and ask them about a topic in my book. I bore friends to death at dinner parties about whatever hare-brained scheme I have up my sleeve. It becomes a part of me.

This is what I want for you, too.

People like to hear what others are doing when it's a kooky project. I especially love the reaction, complete with a head shake and maybe even one eye partly closed, "I'm sorry, what did you say you were working on?"

Go ahead, try it.

Tell people you're doing one of these things:

1. I have a new project at work. Want to see the PowerPoint?
2. My day today was just like my day yesterday. Should I elaborate?
3. Hey there! I wanted to tell you about that same thing I told you about last time but in more detail. Do you have a spare four hours?

Or you could try this:

1. My daughter and I are doing an experiment to write the worst children's book in the state of Wisconsin. It's about gopher poop worms. Want to see the cover?
2. My son said dogs can talk and he's writing a book about it. It's 13 pages and it's called, "No, I Don't Have to Pee."
3. My 9-year-old daughter is doing research on 9-year-old

girls who can tell stories with their eyes closed. Is Megan here today?

Maybe they'll ask you to step away from the cookie jar. Maybe they'll reconsider the ski weekend plans they had and forget to call you.

But maybe you'll strike a nerve. Maybe you'll make a connection. Maybe you'll make a scene and they'll want to be a part of it.

Maybe nothing will come of it.

Maybe something will come of it.

How are we going to know if we don't experiment?

In the next chapters, I've placed articles that I published over the past four years that have helped me build Spark to what it is today. Maybe they'll be a match to your Spark and ignite some creativity in you and your kids and get this party started.

34

HOW TO INSTILL CREATIVITY IN YOUR CHILDREN IN THREE NOT-SO-EASY STEPS.

YOU'D LIKE YOUR CHILD TO THINK, TO EXPLORE, TO IMAGINE AND CREATE. IT MIGHT TAKE A BIT OF HEAVY LIFTING.

"It's really difficult working with kids and with babies because they are not cooperative subjects: they are not socialized into the idea that they should cheerfully and cooperatively give you information. They're not like undergraduates, who you can bribe with beer money or course credit."

— Paul Bloom

*H*eavy lifting? Know anyone with a crane?
Lucky for you, I don't give up easily. In fact, I don't give up at all.

- **Goal:** to get my son and his friend to work on a story for the upcoming (illustrated!) next book in the Li & Lu series.
- **Challenge:** he doesn't wanna.

I had asked my son numerous times to "work on his story" with his friend. I knew I needed to ask in a different way (like not use the word "work" or "story" or make a direct request...). I needed to somehow make it more interesting, but I wasn't finding the right connection. He wasn't annoyed with me, he just wasn't excited about it.

I needed a new tactic.

Don't give up. You, hopefully, have more staying power than your kids. You can outlast their stubbornness. Besides, it's for their benefit for you to win this one.

How to recruit your creative team, embrace technology, and squash writer's block.

I needed to find someone who wasn't me. Someone to give the kids just that little head start from which they could continue on. I needed some fresh blood.

I combined several new approaches that I decided to try out.

1. **Friend's mother:** my son and her own son love her. I need her help.
2. **Techno-bribery:** the boys love being on a computer or tablet. I could fall back on my trusty Google Docs and use that as bait to lure them in.
3. **Kill the blank page:** the blank page can be scary and intimidating. Creating from nothing can be stressful. So I started their story for them.

I created a shared Google document and invited my son and his friend to share the document. I also talked to my son's friend's (his name is Toto in the book) mom and ask for her help. She texted me later that afternoon that the shared thing didn't work. It sounded like they weren't going to try to take it any further.

I pushed.

I invited her email address to the shared doc and asked again (read: pleaded) to just try to get them to work on it for 10 minutes. She said she would. I didn't hear anything more about it that day.

The next day, my son said, in passing, in his nonchalant way, "Oh yeah, we worked on it. We finished it."

Wait, what? You did what? You really did? You worked on it together with Toto? You finished?

For the record and for the jury to hear the evidence, I'm just going to highlight those words yet again:

- "We worked on it"
- "We finished it"

(Thank you for your patience, it'll help with the trial later on how they actually did work and finished things.)

They really had worked on it and finished it.

I jumped on my computer and there it was: the shared document with the opening scene of a story was worked on and finished. I read it and was surprised when I laughed out loud at the ending. They did it! They worked together on it and typed and created the end of the story–and it was funny!

The not-so-secret motive behind writing a book with your kids.

I'm not terribly interested in writing the great American novel. I'm not fascinated by the best-seller list. Sure, those are great and I'd love to achieve that (and, actually, I will), but my goals are parallel to those:

- I want to give my kids the gift of creativity.
- I want them to be able to create something from nothing.
- I want them to start and finish a project and own it.
- I want them to be proud of what they did.
- I want them to feel confident in their next project.
- I want them to want their next project to be better than their first and if it isn't, to work on a third project.
- I want to get the ball rolling.
- I want to be the spark.

I succeeded. They succeeded. We succeeded.

35

LOSS LEADERS, SALES, FLEA MARKETS AND 12-YEAR OLDS WHO WANT NEW SHOES.
YOU CAN CALL IT MATH OR YOU CAN CALL IT CURRENCY TO BUY FROZEN SLUSHIES. UP TO YOU.

"'Priced to sell' - just the phrase makes me smile. When a dealer says all the items in his booth are priced to sell, he means he's tagged them as aggressively as he can to get you to buy them. Don't worry, though, I still haggle. You have to. That's the point of a flea market."

— Nate Berkus

*Y*ou can hang out with your kids at the park. Or you can hang out with your kids at the park and (secretly) teach them about sales, marketing, and economics.

I can't help it. I'm kind of addicted to teaching my kids at every occasion where I see an opportunity. Which is pretty much all the time. We were at a (sort of) flea market this afternoon. Which, in case you didn't know, is an entire self-contained economic ecosystem.

Requirements: In order for your child to learn, they must want something. Children (well, adults too) usually want something, you just have to figure out what it is. It's usually not that hard: just ask. My 12-year old wants new shoes. He has plenty of shoes, but he wants more shoes. A "luxury" expense so he has to earn his own money for it. He's *motivated*.

Motivation is powerful.

The Economic Environment (AKA the Flea Market)

My boys can't get enough of Donald Duck books. We have hundreds. Well, we had hundreds. We must have sold a hundred today.

But not everyone is a fan of the Donald Duck comic books (yet!). Especially the younger kids probably don't know about them--especially if they can't read. But the Duck books were the bulk of what we were trying to sell today at King's Day (a huge event which celebrates the Dutch king's birthday, although it's really the Queen's birthday, but that's yet another Dutch thing). We needed to get those kids to little kids to our books. Enter the Loss Leader.

> "A loss leader is a pricing strategy where a product is sold at a price below its market cost to stimulate other sales of more profitable goods or services."
>
> — WIKIPEDIA

We just happened to have boxes (and boxes) of plastic garbage (also known as little kid toys). We had hard plastic dinosaurs, Matchbox cars, toy trains and a plethora of worthless trinkets. In other words, a little kid magnet. Their parents can't hold them back, they're drawn to them like a comet to the sun.

We strategically placed our ocean-polluting figurines at the edges of our blanketed shop to suck in the innocent buyers. It worked like magic. We had kids practically brawling over a plastic Godzilla that was missing a wing.

The parents had no choice but to hang around and hover over their child while they sorted through horses, whales and cars. Have you ever closely watched kids looking through toys? It's truly a thing of joy. They are mesmerized. A meteor could strike the neighboring blanket and the jolt to the planet might only make them flinch to the point where they drop the petroleum-based giraffe and pick up the 3-wheeled train car.

Unless mom and dad are being called away to speak at the United Nations, they're sticking around until Junior decides between the purple camel and the naturally-weapon-heavy stegosaurus. They can't say no. In fact, you can help them to not say no by making the kid catnip absolutely...free.

Boom and just like that you understand what a Loss Leader is. Pretty fun stuff, right? This is how I explained it to my 12-year old today in play-by-play action-packed commentary. Wait, it gets better.

BONUS: if you happen to have a 10-year old around, put them to work as a "greeter." Let them charm mom and dad by talking about how he played with the pterodactyl and it possibly altered the path of his life's purpose. He should be cute and barely make eye contact with adults and mostly focus on doing tricks with his kendama. Gets 'em every time.

So while Junior is in a heated discussion (with himself) about which animal to take home and cherish until death do they part, mom and dad are checking out what else is on offer. What else is on offer is a huge variety of educational material that could propel Junior to reading at a high-school level after just 27 (low-cost) Donald Ducks. And guess what? We just happen to have at least 27 Donald Ducks available for immediate purchase and delivery. No shipping and handling fees!

With that free Loss Leader securely in Junior's iron-fisted grip, the deal is just about done. A cocktail of guilt, education reform and that-10-year-old-was-so-sweet-to-Junior-we-have-to-buy-a-few-books and mom and dad are picking up their new favorite comic book series. At least two, sometimes four or five, one guy bought a box of Donald Ducks and an entire collection of Dolfje Weerwolfje.

Did you follow what happened here? We gave away a free plastic dinosaur and made a multiple-unit sale.

Let's summarize the entire transaction. Because there's a lot going on.

1. The **kid** is thrilled with his plastic whatever that he'll probably lose before he gets home. But he has the memory of a goldfish so he's just inherently happy and will have forgotten about the entire day by then anyway and will just wonder when dinner is.
2. We've supplied the **parents** with enough reading material to read to their son in bed for the next three years. Value? Eternal and limitless joy. Score!
3. My **10-year old** helped a little boy choose his gift and built his own confidence as he felt useful to the small boy. He's smiling and proud.
4. My **12-year old** is $14 closer to the new shoes he doesn't need.
5. I got rid of four pounds of books we've read 87 times each and I got to teach my kids about economics.

Let me count: that's win + win + win + win + win.

We're not even to the best part. All of this doesn't even come close to what really happened here.

Today I got to:

1. talk to my boys,
2. hang out with them in the park in the sun and drink overly sugary drinks that they're never allowed to have,
3. teach them what I know without them knowing that I was teaching them anything.

We didn't sit down and use paper or calculators. There wasn't a textbook anywhere. We joked about which kids were going to see the dinosaurs. We were **learning by experience.** We were instilling knowledge into their brains by doing, through real-life situations with real money and real people. We didn't know the outcome of any transaction beforehand so there was the element of adventure and risk.

If I improved their lives just a smidgen, it's a good day.

If they learned something through experience, it's a great day.

It's just a single day, just a day like any other, but I taught my boys something and that's the biggest win.

I am 100% certain my boys would have no idea what I'm going on and on about here, maybe they will when they hit university. But I have the biggest smile on my face as I write this because today was both just another day and yet it was the greatest day. It's possible to make it both.

What are you going to do with a regular Saturday? It's up to you.

36

MAKE MONEY, TEACH YOUR KIDS MATH, AND CLEAN THE HOUSE...AT THE SAME TIME.

WHAT IF VACUUMING WERE A SPORT? WITH PRIZES?

"In my school, the brightest boys did math and physics, the less bright did physics and chemistry, and the least bright did biology. I wanted to do math and physics, but my father made me do chemistry because he thought there would be no jobs for mathematicians."

— STEPHEN HAWKING

*M*ake money? Teach math? Clean the house? At the same time? (Gather up thick French accent:) Impossible!

In fact, some days, any of those alone seem impossible.

You just need to get creative.

The challenge: we need to clean the house before we leave tomorrow and the kids need to help. It's not going to be fun. Oh yeah, they need to study math. Making money would be fun, but sounds like a long shot.

Here's the Deal

Whenever "work" or "study" or "learning" is even whispered, the kids seem to magically come down with acute cases of deafness, miraculous whole-body paralysis, and calls for emergency bowel movements. They'll say anything. But too bad for them, we need to get out of this house and it needs to be done. We also need to learn some math.

The Goals

Clean the house (no, ALL of us).
    Learn math (4th & 6th grade). We're going for functions today such as: sum, percentage, and differences.
    Make money in the process (that one is up to me, you'll see).
    Forget studying math, let's use math to learn it. Don't even use the word study. It's taboo. What a concept. Let's even throw in how to build and use a spreadsheet, how to look at statistics, and for a bonus: let it do things that are hard to do in our heads (like comparison graphs).

Clean the House

Kids are good with tasks and lists and especially crossing things off lists when we're done. We almost started with a pad of paper this morning, but I decided to go use Google Sheets (Google's version of spreadsheets) to build a spreadsheet and make charts and graphs. More on that below under Making Money.
    But I mention it because it helps with motivation. They like to see a list, they like to see it being shortened (or crossed off or checked). I figured out how to make a pie chart with tasks completed and not yet completed so they could see progress.
    Imagine this, dear parent friend: together we typed up the list (it's in Dutch in the image but you get the idea) and in order to mark a task from "Nee" to "Ja" (No to Yes on the completed column), my son

raced off to pack his suitcase. Let me repeat those words as I don't write them often. I'll even bold them:

"...my son raced off to pack his suitcase."

If you're a parent of young blobs, you'll be happy enough already. But wait, it gets better.

Learn Math

Disclaimer: I was a math major. I like math. I like the yes and no, right or wrong of it. I think it's fun. I apologize to those in advance who thought math was daily torture. It can be fun!

My kids also like math...they just don't really know what it is in real life. They secretly like it as long as we don't call it math. Enter our spreadsheet of hours and tasks. Just a bunch of numbers, right? Boooooorrrrriiiiinnnnnnggggg! How about a chart? How about a chart of the percentage of tasks completed that changes automatically when we mark a task completed?

Trust me, dear non-math-loving parent, kids like progress. Especially seeing it visually.

Word Problems

Wow, I'm truly my father's son. I actually asked my son this today as we were getting started:

"Yes, there are 12 hours of work, but those are "man hours." If we split them up among the 4 of us, how many hours does each of need to work?"

He was thrilled with the answer (it's 3 in case you skipped 5th grade division).

"So we only have to work 3 hours each and we'll be done? Let's get started!"

I need to apologize again as I don't hear this too much in my house when it comes to actual work:

"Let's get started!" quoted 11-year old when he figured out that he didn't need to individually work 12 hours, but only 3.

I probably went a little overboard with my columns "Estimated Time Worked" and "Actual Time Worked" but I wanted them (and me) to have an idea of what we estimated a task would take and how long it actually took. It was pretty difficult to explain that I had to add a half an hour of my time to helping my son put new sheets on the beds because he needed help with the fitted sheets. So he still worked an hour, but I had to add a half an hour to my time (also increasing the total time worked).

Make Money

I'm a big fan of Google Apps. For example, their documents app (Google Docs) and their spreadsheets (Google Sheets). It's what I used to build the spreadsheet and embedded charts and graphs in our work today. Some time ago, Google approached me because I had promoted their Google Apps for your own domain so much and had so many people sign up with them that they supplied me with coupon codes for Google Apps.

If you know and use Gmail, you know that it's free and you also get all of those Google Apps for free. The difference is that your email address is yourname@gmail.com. With Google Apps for your domain, your email address is you@yourdomain.com. I like this because for our personal addresses, I have my whole family on there and we can easily share things like spreadsheets and documents (we also did my 11-year-old's book report on Google Apps tonight) and they're all under our domain name with our unique email addresses. I just think it's more professional (not to mention long term) to have you@yourdomain.com rather than yourdorkynickname2012@gmail.com.

Another disclaimer: yes, I'm going to make money cleaning the house and teaching my kids math. How do you make money? It's just getting creative with how you do things and how you teach others. How could you help them and make a buck at the same time? In the ideal situation, they're thankful you gave them a tool to achieve something and you make a bit of (kinda) passive income.

Google Apps costs $50 per year per user. But you're probably paying that if you pay for email somewhere else. I have coupons that save 20% ("If the full cost is $50 per year, what does it cost if there is a savings of 20%?"...it's down to $40) per user per year for the first year.

If you'd like to sign up for Google Apps so you too can clean your house and teach your kids math, here's your coupon for Google Apps. [update: I think I still have some coupon codes lying around if you really want one, just ask me]

Actual Results

It's now 8 PM and somehow 12 hours divided by 4 didn't equal 3. Maybe we need to revise the spreadsheet. That's OK, my son now knows how to do that. In fact, he's been working on the spreadsheet more than he was working on vacuuming. One last quote just to make me happy and remember this day:

> " ... he's been working on the spreadsheet."

In the long run, I'm happier that he's learning how to work a spreadsheet and also what the charts and graphs do and how to read them. It's a trade-off any parent wouldn't mind: learning math for vacuuming?

This is exactly my goal: doing one thing while (secretly?) learning another without reminding them they're learning something. See how that worked?

On that note, I'll go finishing vacuuming the bedroom because even though Einstein and Descartes have sorta finished their "math" for the day, we didn't actually finish cleaning up.

It's the price I pay for being the Spark for my kids.

HOW WOULD YOUR OWN KID SELL HIS OWN BOOK?
ONCE THE BOOK IS DONE, THE REAL CREATIVITY MIGHT TAKE ROOT.

"Logic will get you from A to B. Imagination will take you everywhere."

— ALBERT EINSTEIN

How do your kids find the books they read? How can they apply that to selling their own book?

I asked my boys on our now famous 12-block walk home from school, "So when the book is out, how should we promote it?"

My 9-year old is not usually motivated by money, but was inspired when we sold a bunch of stuff on Craigslist this weekend and since he helped clean things up, he got a cut of the profits.

Working on your "book project" doesn't only mean fleshing out character traits and plot lines. Get them into the promotion of the book and see what they come up with.

I started early in the walk so we'd have time for lots of ideas. The dog ate some poop along the way, so it threw off our concentration, but by the time we got to Kite Hill, we were rolling in ideas (not poop).

I'm going to get this more or less in their words below.

Li's 5 Best Ways to Promote your Book

1. **Tell everyone in your class.** Get your friends to buy it.
2. **Make a book trailer.** A short film about the book. (Li didn't say "book trailer" but he said something like a short film about the book and the characters).
3. **Create a print book version.** Because more people read paper than on a Kindle.
4. **Make a Kindle version.** Because Li has a Kindle and it's easy to buy books on it (Editor's note: a little too easy, in fact).
5. **Pay for ads.** "But it's really expensive," Li added. We talked about how it depends on where it's advertised. Maybe if it's in their school newsletter, not so much, but more if it's the San Francisco Chronicle.

Lu's 5 Top Ways to Promote your Book

1. **Make a movie.** Get it on Netflix. "That way, everyone can see it." We talked about how this might be quite an undertaking ...
2. **Make an ad.** Can make a little video and put it on YouTube. Just a thing that says, "It's awesome."
3. **Back cover blurb.** Based on what Lu said, this sounds like a blurb, why the book is so good, a little bit about it.
4. **Funny examples of book on back cover.** Lu showed me the back of his Big Nate books when we got home and they do a very animated job of promotion: examples from the book, promotional blurbs, even little incomplete lists that you can fill out. Fun stuff!
5. **Bribery.** Give some extra money to the people who work at the book store so they put it at the front of the store.

(Editor's note: I am laughing out loud as I write this as I love that he thought of this on his own!)

How would your kids promote what you worked on together? Think they never think about this stuff? Well, maybe they don't, but if you ask them and give them a few blocks of walking (and few other distractions), they might surprise you.

PART VII

GLOW

"Success consists of going from failure to failure without loss of enthusiasm."

— Winston Churchill

38

SPARK CAMPFIRE
BEYOND THE BOOK

> "Every successful individual knows that his or her achievement depends on a community of persons working together."
>
> — Paul Ryan

There is a Spark world beyond these pages. It's called Spark Campfire not only to continue on my whole sparks and kindling and fire analogies, but because I see it as a community coming together and sharing stories.

Here's a bullet list of words that come to mind when I think of what Spark Campfire will become:

1. community
2. stories
3. collections
4. laughing
5. contests for the worst 14-page book of all time
6. marshmallows
7. cooperation
8. co-creating

9. tears of frustration
10. tears of joy
11. audiobook chapters recorded by kids
12. a mom's first novel
13. a dad's dream come true
14. uncles who write books with their nieces
15. stuff I can't even imagine here
16. adventure
17. play

I tend to see things visually. I get these movie scenes in my mind and it's often how I write—I just get down what I see as fast as I can in words.

The visuals keep coming and when I have this, I know I'm usually onto something. I see more of them.

I see kids laughing at their parents (as well as with them).

A mother crying because her daughter was more creative than they ever imagined and telling her story opened up a part of her she hadn't ever witnessed.

An uncle who gets to know his niece better.

A young author who finally has an audience—her parents.

Strangers helping other strangers promote each other's books.

Maybe a grandma helping out her son who's helping out his niece.

A young boy who comes out of his shell and spills his imagination onto the page.

I see lots of things in Spark Campfire. What might you see?

If there are marshmallows, we might even get Li & Lu to visit.

Want to be a part of it? Come see what we're cooking up over at spark.repossible.com.

39

QUESTIONS FOR PARENTS
PRETEND IT'S CAMP AND YOU CAN ASK ANYTHING

"You ask me a question. I have a blank mind. You ask me a question, and the question is informed, and you're interested, and now my mind starts popping. That's what conversation is. That's what communicating is."

— Melissa Leo

This book is not just a book. Well, sure, what you have in your hands is a book, but that's like saying you have a match in your hand and paper in the other.

Stuff is going to happen.

1. I have questions. You have answers.
2. You have questions. I have answers.

What happened with you? Care to share?

Here are some questions I'd love to hear your answers to—as would others who are stuck or recently unstuck.

1. What sparked the initial interest?

2. How did you create and develop your child's interest in this project?
3. What hesitations did you and your kids have to overcome?
4. How did you negotiate, navigate, and partner through the creative process?
5. What were the sticking points that slowed or stalled the process? How did you overcome them?
6. How did everyone view the end product of your collective work?

AFTERWORD

Just after we finished "The Secret of Kite Hill" and I talked about what the boys and I had done I planned to write this book.

It's been 4 years.

I would say "I can't believe I finally did it." except that I can believe it.

Because ever since "Every Single Day," I just get stuff done.

Maybe not fast, maybe not perfect, but I'll get it done.

Spark is now a thing. It's done. It's here.

I'm ready for it to come to life.

I hope you'll share it with me.

ACKNOWLEDGMENTS

This book was the biggest collaborative effort I've ever been a part of.

My mantra for 2018 was Better Together and I can now say with all confidence that things are certainly better together.

I couldn't have done this without the help, stories, and generosity from:

- Rina Mae Acosta
- Arlene Pe Benito
- Maggie Daniels
- Colleen Golafshan
- Linda Hamilton
- Meg Leal
- Adwynna MacKenzie
- Lizz Mendez
- Matt Michel
- John Muldoon
- Gavin Reese
- Rich Robinson
- Brad Silverman
- Lorena Veldhuijzen

- Craig Young

But what's fun about Spark is that this book isn't the end. There is so much more we can play with. I see this list growing with more families and stories and the unknown.

Maybe you'll be next?

RELATIONSHIP

Building a relationship with readers is one of the best things about writing.

I occasionally send an email with details about **new books, sneak peeks** into Works In Progress, early bird **deals**, as well as exclusive, **Readers Only insights** into the writing and publishing process.

For Spark, it all lights up at spark.repossible.com.

ABOUT THE AUTHOR

Bradley Charbonneau is an "unstoppable writing machine."

He can't not write. Writing gives him pleasure, perspective, and the chance to overuse the letter "p" whenever he feels like it.

He doesn't take himself terribly seriously—except for that daily writing habit he's got going on. He's truly reached Part 7: Glow and isn't heading back down ever again.

All he really wants to do is tell stories, travel with his wife to oddball destinations by rickety transport, shoot baskets with his boys, try to perfect the burrito outside of California, and whisper the secrets of freedom and deep joy to whomever is within earshot and shares even the slightest inkling of curiosity.

He currently lives in a little town outside of Utrecht in The Netherlands with his wife Saskia, famous two young boys of "The Adventures of Li & Lu" fame, and their at-least-as-famous dog Pepper.

This is Bradley's fourteenth book.

It is far, far, far from his last.

Find, ask, discuss, play at:
bradleycharbonneau.com

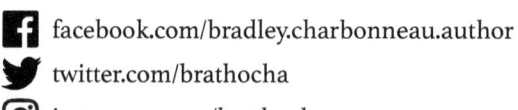

facebook.com/bradley.charbonneau.author
twitter.com/brathocha
instagram.com/brathocha

ALSO BY BRADLEY CHARBONNEAU

Most of my books are also available as audiobooks (which I giddily narrate). Search for my name at your favorite audiobook distributor, slip on your headphones, and let me take you away.

Repossible

Repossible

Every Single Day (+ Playbook)

Ask

Dare

Create

Decide

Meditate

Spark

Surrender

Play

Elevate

Frequency

Every Single Day

Every Single Day Playbook

Every Single Day Kids

Every Single Day Teens (I want to write this one because I want to read this one...)

Every Single Day Parents

Charlie Holiday

Now Is Your Chance (1)

Second Chance (2)

Chance of a Lifetime (3)

For Creatives

Audio for Authors

Meditation for Creatives (2020)

Shorts

Secret Bus to Paradise

Where I (Already) Am

Pass the Sour Cream

A Trip to Hel

Drive-By Dropping

Li & Lu

The Secret of Kite Hill (1)

The Secret of Markree Castle (2)

The Key to Markree Castle (3)

The Gift of Markree Castle (4)

Driehoek (5)

Really Old …

urban travel guide SAN FRANCISCO

THE END

Thank you for reading "Spark."
   Books don't often have "The End" anymore, so I thought I'd make sure we're really done here.
   But of course it's just the beginning.
   I hope to see you around the campfire where we can see what lights up, warm up around the fire, and get our glow on.

AFTERWORD

We have now Decided, we Meditated (and will continue to do so... right?) and Sparked energy in others.

What's next?

- Surrender
- Play
- Celebrate

Thanks you for reading. We're in the thick of it now but it's getting easier and will only get easier, more fun, and powerful.

Bradley Charbonneau